W. H. Withrow

A Harmony of the Gospels

W. H. Withrow

A Harmony of the Gospels

ISBN/EAN: 9783744648516

Printed in Europe, USA, Canada, Australia, Japan

Cover: Foto ©Thomas Meinert / pixelio.de

More available books at **www.hansebooks.com**

A HARMONY OF THE GOSPELS

BEING THE

LIFE OF JESUS

IN THE WORDS OF THE FOUR EVANGELISTS.

ARRANGED BY

W. H. WITHROW, D.D., F.R.S.C.

From the Revised Version of the New Testament.

TORONTO:

WILLIAM BRIGGS.

Montreal: C. W. COATES. Halifax: S. F. HUESTIS.

1894.

PREFACE.

THE purpose of the compiler of this HARMONY OF THE GOSPELS has been to so interweave the narratives of the four Evangelists as to give as full and flowing an account as possible of the life of our Lord. He has therefore sought to bring into the text every sentence, indeed every word, which could add to the completeness of the record. The footnote references will show how intricate this interweaving in many cases has been; and a careful examination will show what increased light the introduction of even a single word from a parallel account will give. In a few instances, however, to secure the completeness sought, the different accounts of the same event are repeated in full, as in the narrative of the institution of the Lord's Supper, the denial of Peter, the resurrection of Jesus, and a few others. In a few instances these, for the sake of clearness, are printed in parallel columns, and are sometimes enclosed in brackets. The two versions of the Sermon on the Mount are given in full, for reasons indicated in a footnote.

The advantage of such a Harmony, or Monotessaron, will be shown by the following extracts from an article by Prof. Amos R. Wells, in the *Sunday-school Times:*

"Far above Concordance, Bible Index, Bible Dictionary, I count the Monotessaron the very best help to Bible study. The Monotessaron, it might be parenthetically remarked for the benefit of the lexicon-lazy folk, is a Harmony of the four Gospels so arranged as to make one continuous and complete story, in Scripture words alone. Speaking for one, I may say that through recent first acquaintance with a Monotessaron, that matchless life has shone upon me with an entire splendor of beauty and majesty before unimagined.

"A further inestimable advantage is the appreciation of surroundings. What light is cast, for example, on the story of Lazarus in John by its insertion in Luke; the contact of these parted elements of the Gospel story sometimes rouses a current of thrilling thoughts, making a veritable electric battery of the Monotessaron.

"It has given the life and person of Christ marvellous vividness, setting facts in their due order, location, relations and proportions, while the facility it affords is constant inspiration to fresh delightful study. This is the experience of thousands, and yet I am sure that there are many thousands who are yet unacquainted with this Bible-help. Not only every Sunday-school teacher, but every Bible scholar should own one."

That this HARMONY OF THE GOSPELS may make the life of our Lord a more vivid reality and abiding power in the hearts of its readers is the earnest prayer of

THE EDITOR.

CONTENTS.

vi Contents.

A HARMONY OF THE GOSPELS.

§ 1—ST. JOHN'S INTRODUCTION.

In the beginning was the Word, and the Word was with God, and the Word was God. The same was in the beginning with God. All things were made by him; and without him was not anything made that hath been made. In him was life; and the life was the light of men. And the light shineth in the darkness; and the darkness apprehended it not. There came a man, sent from God, whose name was John. The same came for witness, that he might bear witness of the light, that all might believe through him. He was not the light, but *came* that he might bear witness of the light. There was the true light, *even the light* which lighteth every man, coming into the world. He was in the world, and the world was made by him, and the world knew him not. He came unto his own, and they that were his own received him not. But as many as received him, to them gave he the right to become children of God, *even* to them that believe on his name: which were born, not of blood, nor of the will of the flesh, nor of the will of man, but of God. And the Word became flesh, and dwelt among us (and we beheld his glory, glory as of the only begotten from the Father), full of grace and truth. John beareth witness of him, and crieth, saying, This was he of whom I said, He that cometh after me is become before me: for he was before me. For of his fulness we all received, and grace for grace. For the law was given by Moses; grace and truth came by Jesus Christ. No man hath seen God at any time; the only begotten Son, which is in the bosom of the Father, he hath declared *him*.[1]

---

1. John 1 : 1-18.

2   *A Harmony of the Gospels.*

§2—THE GENEALOGY OF JESUS.

The book of the generation of Jesus Christ, the son of David, the son of Abraham.

Abraham begat Isaac; and Isaac begat Jacob; and Jacob begat Judah and his brethren; and Judah begat Perez and Zerah of Tamar; and Perez begat Hezron; and Hezron begat Ram; and Ram begat Amminadab; and Amminadab begat Nahshon; and Nahshon begat Salmon; and Salmon begat Boaz of Rahab; and Boaz begat Obed of Ruth; and Obed begat Jesse; and Jesse begat David the king.

And David begat Solomon of her *that had been the wife* of Uriah; and Solomon begat Rehoboam; and Rehoboam begat Abijah; and Abijah begat Asa; and Asa begat Jehoshaphat; and Jehoshaphat begat Joram; and Joram begat Uzziah; and Uzziah begat Jotham; and Jotham begat Ahaz; and Ahaz begat Hezekiah; and Hezekiah begat Manasseh; and Manasseh begat Amon; and Amon begat Josiah; and Josiah begat Jechoniah and his brethren, at the time of the carrying away to Babylon.

And after the carrying away to Babylon, Jechoniah begat Shealtiel; and Shealtiel begat Zerubbabel; and Zerubbabel begat Abiud; and Abiud begat Eliakim; and Eliakim begat Azor; and Azor begat Sadoc; and Sadoc begat Achim; and Achim begat Eliud; and Eliud begat Eleazar; and Eleazar begat Matthan; and Matthan begat Jacob; and Jacob begat Joseph the husband of Mary, of whom was born Jesus, who is called Christ.

So all the generations from Abraham unto David are fourteen generations; and from David unto the carrying away to Babylon fourteen generations; and from the carrying away to Babylon unto the Christ fourteen generations.[1]

And Jesus himself, when he began *to teach*, was about thirty years of age, being the son (as was supposed) of Joseph, the *son* of Heli, the *son* of Matthat, the *son* of Levi, the *son* of Melchi, the *son* of Jannai, the *son* of Joseph, the

---

1. Matt. 1 : 1-17.

son of Mattathias, the *son* of Amos, the *son* of Nahum, the son of Esli, the *son* of Naggai, the *son* of Maath, the *son* of Mattathias, the *son* of Semein, the *son* of Josech, the *son* of Joda, the *son* of Joanan, the *son* of Rhesa, the *son* of Zerubbabel, the *son* of Shealtiel, the *son* of Neri, the *son* of Melchi, the *son* of Addi, the *son* of Cosam, the *son* of Elmadam, the *son* of Er, the *son* of Jesus, the *son* of Eliezer, the *son* of Jorim, the *son* of Matthat, the *son* of Levi, the *son* of Symeon, the *son* of Judas, the *son* of Joseph, the *son* of Jonam, the *son* of Eliakim, the *son* of Melea, the *son* of Menna, the *son* of Mattatha, the *son* of Nathan, the *son* of David, the *son* of Jesse, the *son* of Obed, the *son* of Boaz, the *son* of Salmon, the *son* of Nahshon, the *son* of Amminadab, the *son* of Arni, the *son* of Hezron, the *son* of Perez, the *son* of Judah, the *son* of Jacob, the *son* of Isaac, the *son* of Abraham, the *son* of Terah, the *son* of Nahor, the *son* of Serug, the *son* of Reu, the *son* of Peleg, the *son* of Eber, the *son* of Shelah, the *son* of Cainan, the *son* of Arphaxad, the *son* of Shem, the *son* of Noah, the *son* of Lamech, the *son* of Methuselah, the *son* of Enoch, the *son* of Jared, the *son* of Mahalaleel, the *son* of Cainan, the *son* of Enos, the *son* of Seth, the *son* of Adam, the *son* of God.[1]

§3—THE ANNUNCIATION OF THE BIRTH OF JOHN AND OF JESUS.

There was in the days of Herod, king of Judæa, a certain priest named Zacharias, of the course of Abijah: and he had a wife of the daughters of Aaron, and her name was Elisabeth. And they were both righteous before God, walking in all the commandments and ordinances of the Lord blameless. And they had no child, because that Elisabeth was barren, and they both were *now* well stricken in years.

Now it came to pass, while he executed the priest's office before God in the order of his course, according to the custom of the priest's office, his lot was to enter into the temple of the Lord and burn incense. And the whole multitude of[2]

---

1. Luke 3 : 23-38.   2. Luke 1 : 5-10.

the people were praying without at the hour of incense. And there appeared unto him an angel of the Lord standing on the right side of the altar of incense. And Zacharias was troubled when he saw *him*, and fear fell upon him. But the angel said unto him, Fear not, Zacharias: because thy supplication is heard, and thy wife Elisabeth shall bear thee a son, and thou shalt call his name John. And thou shalt have joy and gladness; and many shall rejoice at his birth. For he shall be great in the sight of the Lord, and he shall drink no wine nor strong drink; and he shall be filled with the Holy Ghost, even from his mother's womb. And many of the children of Israel shall he turn unto the Lord their God. And he shall go before his face in the spirit and power of Elijah, to turn the hearts of the fathers to the children, and the disobedient *to walk* in the wisdom of the just; to make ready for the Lord a people prepared *for him*. And Zacharias said unto the angel, Whereby shall I know this? for I am an old man, and my wife well stricken in years. And the angel answering said unto him, I am Gabriel, that stand in the presence of God; and I was sent to speak unto thee, and to bring thee these good tidings. And behold, thou shalt be silent and not able to speak, until the day that these things shall come to pass, because thou believedst not my words, which shall be fulfilled in their season. And the people were waiting for Zacharias, and they marvelled while he tarried in the temple. And when he came out, he could not speak unto them: and they perceived that he had seen a vision in the temple: and he continued making signs unto them, and remained dumb. And it came to pass, when the days of his ministration were fulfilled, he departed unto his house.

And after these days Elisabeth his wife conceived; and she hid herself five months, saying, Thus hath the Lord done unto me in the days wherein he looked upon *me*, to take away my reproach among men.

Now in the sixth month the angel Gabriel was sent from God unto a city of Galilee, named Nazareth, to a virgin[1]

---

1. Luke 1 : 10-27.

betrothed to a man whose name was Joseph, of the house of David; and the virgin's name was Mary. And he came in unto her, and said, Hail, thou that art highly favoured, the Lord *is* with thee. But she was greatly troubled at the saying, and cast in her mind what manner of salutation this might be. And the angel said unto her, Fear not, Mary: for thou hast found favour with God. And behold, thou shalt conceive in thy womb, and bring forth a son, and shalt call his name JESUS. He shall be great, and shall be called the Son of the Most High: and the Lord God shall give unto him the throne of his father David: and he shall reign over the house of Jacob for ever; and of his kingdom there shall be no end. And Mary said unto the angel, How shall this be, seeing I know not a man? And the angel answered and said unto her, The Holy Ghost shall come upon thee, and the power of the Most High shall overshadow thee: wherefore also that which is to be born shall be called holy, the Son of God. And behold, Elisabeth thy kinswoman, she also hath conceived a son in her old age: and this is the sixth month with her that was called barren. For no word from God shall be void of power. And Mary said, Behold, the handmaid of the Lord; be it unto me according to thy word. And the angel departed from her.

And Mary arose in these days and went into the hill country with haste, into a city of Judah; and entered into the house of Zacharias and saluted Elisabeth. And it came to pass, when Elisabeth heard the salutation of Mary, the babe leaped in her womb; and Elisabeth was filled with the Holy Ghost; and she lifted up her voice with a loud cry, and said, Blessed *art* thou among women, and blessed *is* the fruit of thy womb. And whence is this to me, that the mother of my Lord should come unto me? For behold, when the voice of thy salutation came into mine ears, the babe leaped in my womb for joy. And blessed *is* she that believed; for there shall be a fulfilment of the things which have been spoken to her from the Lord. And Mary said,

My soul doth magnify the Lord,
And my spirit hath rejoiced in God my Saviour.[1]

---

[1]. Luke 1: 27-47.

For he hath looked upon the low estate of his hand-
    maiden:
For behold, from henceforth all generations shall call
    me blessed.
For he that is mighty hath done to me great things;
And holy is his name.
And his mercy is unto generations and generations
On them that fear him.
He hath shewed strength with his arm;
He hath scattered the proud in the imagination of their
    heart.
He hath put down princes from *their* thrones,
And hath exalted them of low degree.
The hungry he hath filled with good things;
And the rich he hath sent empty away.
He hath holpen Israel his servant,
That he might remember mercy
(As he spake unto our fathers)
Toward Abraham and his seed for ever.

And Mary abode with her about three months, and returned unto her house.[1]

§4—THE BIRTH OF JOHN.

Now Elisabeth's time was fulfilled that she should be
delivered; and she brought forth a son. And her neighbours and her kinsfolk heard that the Lord had magnified
his mercy towards her; and they rejoiced with her. And it
came to pass on the eighth day, that they came to circumcise
the child; and they would have called him Zacharias, after
the name of his father. And his mother answered and said,
Not so; but he shall be called John. And they said unto
her, There is none of thy kindred that is called by this
name. And they made signs to his father, what he would
have him called. And he asked for a writing tablet, and
wrote, saying, His name is John. And they marvelled all.
And his mouth was opened immediately, and his tongue[2]

---

1. Luke 1: 48-56.   2. Luke 1: 57-64.

loosed, and he spake, blessing God. And fear came on all that dwelt round about them: and all these sayings were noised abroad throughout all the hill country of Judæa. And all that heard them laid them up in their heart, saying, What then shall this child be? For the hand of the Lord was with him.

And his father Zacharias was filled with the Holy Ghost, and prophesied, saying,

Blessed *be* the Lord, the God of Israel;
For he hath visited and wrought redemption for his people,
And hath raised up a horn of salvation for us
In the house of his servant David
(As he spake by the mouth of his holy prophets which have been since the world began),
Salvation from our enemies, and from the hand of all that hate us;
To shew mercy towards our fathers,
And to remember his holy covenant;
The oath which he sware unto Abraham our father,
To grant unto us that we being delivered out of the hand of our enemies
Should serve him without fear,
In holiness and righteousness before him all our days.
Yea and thou, child, shalt be called the prophet of the Most High:
For thou shalt go before the face of the Lord to make ready his ways;
To give knowledge of salvation unto his people
In the remission of their sins,
Because of the tender mercy of our God,
Whereby the dayspring from on high shall visit us,
To shine upon them that sit in darkness and the shadow of death;
To guide our feet into the way of peace.

And the child grew, and waxed strong in spirit, and was in the deserts till the day of his shewing unto Israel.[1]

---

1. Luke 1: 64-80.

§5——THE BIRTH OF JESUS.

Now the birth of Jesus Christ was on this wise: When his mother Mary had been betrothed to Joseph, before they came together she was found with child of the Holy Ghost. And Joseph her husband, being a righteous man, and not willing to make her a public example, was minded to put her away privily. But when he thought on these things, behold, an angel of the Lord appeared unto him in a dream, saying, Joseph, thou son of David, fear not to take unto thee Mary thy wife: for that which is conceived in her is of the Holy Ghost. And she shall bring forth a son; and thou shalt call his name JESUS; for it is he that shall save his people from their sins. Now all this is come to pass, that it might be fulfilled which was spoken by the Lord through the prophet, saying,

Behold, the virgin shall be with child, and shall bring
forth a son,
And they shall call his name Immanuel;

which is, being interpreted, God with us. And Joseph arose from his sleep, and did as the angel of the Lord commanded him, and took unto him his wife; and knew her not till she had brought forth a son: and he called his name JESUS.[1]

Now it came to pass in those days, there went out a decree from Cæsar Augustus, that all the world should be enrolled. This was the first enrolment made when Quirinius was governor of Syria. And all went to enrol themselves, every one to his own city. And Joseph also went up from Galilee, out of the city of Nazareth, into Judæa, to the city of David, which is called Bethlehem, because he was of the house and family of David; to enrol himself with Mary, who was betrothed to him, being great with child. And it came to pass, while they were there, the days were fulfilled that she should be delivered. And she brought forth her firstborn son; and she wrapped him in swaddling clothes, and laid him in a manger, because there was no room for them in the inn.[2]

---

1. Matt. 1: 18-25.   2. Luke 2: 1-7.

And there were shepherds in the same country abiding in the field, and keeping watch by night over their flock.　And an angel of the Lord stood by them, and the glory of the Lord shone round about them : and they were sore afraid. And the angel said unto them, Be not afraid ; for behold, I bring you good tidings of great joy which shall be to all the people : for there is born to you this day in the city of David a Saviour, which is Christ the Lord.　And this *is* the sign unto you ; Ye shall find a babe wrapped in swaddling clothes, and lying in a manger.　And suddenly there was with the angel a multitude of the heavenly host praising God, and saying,

Glory to God in the highest,
And on earth peace among men in whom he is well
　　pleased.

And it came to pass, when the angels went away from them into heaven, the shepherds said one to another, Let us now go even unto Bethlehem, and see this thing that is come to pass, which the Lord hath made known unto us. And they came with haste, and found both Mary and Joseph, and the babe lying in the manger.　And when they saw it, they made known concerning the saying which was spoken to them about this child.　And all that heard it wondered at the things which were spoken unto them by the shepherds. But Mary kept all these sayings, pondering them in her heart.　And the shepherds returned, glorifying and praising God for all the things that they had heard and seen, even as it was spoken unto them.[1]

§6—THE PRESENTATION OF JESUS IN THE
TEMPLE.

And when eight days were fulfilled for circumcising him, his name was called Jesus, which was so called by the angel before he was conceived in the womb.

And when the days of their purification according to the law of Moses were fulfilled, they brought him up to Jerusa-

---

1. Luke 2 : 8-20.

lem, to present him to the Lord (as it is written in the law
of the Lord, Every male that openeth the womb shall be
called holy to the Lord), and to offer a sacrifice according to
that which is said in the law of the Lord, A pair of turtle-
doves, or two young pigeons. And behold, there was a man
in Jerusalem, whose name was Simeon; and this man was
righteous and devout, looking for the consolation of Israel:
and the Holy Spirit was upon him. And it had been revealed unto him by the Holy Spirit, that he should not see
death, before he had seen the Lord's Christ. And he came
in the Spirit into the temple: and when the parents brought
in the child Jesus, that they might do concerning him after
the custom of the law, then he received him into his arms,
and blessed God, and said,

Now lettest thou thy servant depart, O Lord,
According to thy word, in peace;
For mine eyes have seen thy salvation,
Which thou hast prepared before the face of all peoples;
A light for revelation to the Gentiles,
And the glory of thy people Israel.

And his father and his mother were marvelling at the things
which were spoken concerning him; and Simeon blessed
them, and said unto Mary his mother, Behold, this *child* is
set for the falling and rising up of many in Israel; and for a
sign which is spoken against; yea and a sword shall pierce
through thine own soul; that thoughts out of many hearts
may be revealed. And there was one Anna, a prophetess,
the daughter of Phanuel, of the tribe of Asher (she was of a
great age, having lived with a husband seven years from her
virginity, and she had been a widow even for fourscore and
four years), which departed not from the temple, worshipping with fastings and supplications night and day. And
coming up at that very hour she gave thanks unto God, and
spake of him to all them that were looking for the redemption of Jerusalem.[1]

---

1. Luke 2: 21-38.

§7—THE WORSHIP OF THE WISE MEN.

Now when Jesus was born in Bethlehem of Judæa in the days of Herod the king, behold, wise men from the east came to Jerusalem, saying, Where is he that is born King of the Jews? for we saw his star in the east, and are come to worship him. And when Herod the king heard it, he was troubled, and all Jerusalem with him. And gathering together all the chief priests and scribes of the people, he inquired of them where the Christ should be born. And they said unto him, In Bethlehem of Judæa: for thus it is written by the prophet,

And thou Bethlehem, land of Judah,
Art in no wise least among the princes of Judah:
For out of thee shall come forth a governor,
Which shall be shepherd of my people Israel.

Then Herod privily called the wise men, and learned of them carefully what time the star appeared. And he sent them to Bethlehem, and said, Go and search out carefully concerning the young child; and when ye have found *him*, bring me word, that I also may come and worship him. And they, having heard the king, went their way; and lo, the star, which they saw in the east, went before them, till it came and stood over where the young child was. And when they saw the star, they rejoiced with exceeding great joy. And they came into the house and saw the young child with Mary his mother; and they fell down and worshipped him; and opening their treasures they offered unto him gifts, gold and frankincense and myrrh. And being warned *of God* in a dream that they should not return to Herod, they departed into their own country another way.[1]

---

1. Matt. 2: 1-12.

§8—THE FLIGHT INTO EGYPT, MASSACRE OF THE INNOCENTS, AND RETURN TO NAZARETH.

Now when they were departed, behold, an angel of the Lord appeareth to Joseph in a dream, saying, Arise and take the young child and his mother, and flee into Egypt, and be thou there until I tell thee: for Herod will seek the young child to destroy him. And he arose and took the young child and his mother by night, and departed into Egypt; and was there until the death of Herod: that it might be fulfilled which was spoken by the Lord through the prophet, saying, Out of Egypt did I call my son. Then Herod, when he saw that he was mocked of the wise men, was exceeding wroth, and sent forth, and slew all the male children that were in Bethlehem, and in all the borders thereof, from two years old and under, according to the time which he had carefully learned of the wise men. Then was fulfilled that which was spoken by Jeremiah the prophet, saying,

A voice was heard in Ramah,
Weeping and great mourning,
Rachel weeping for her children;
And she would not be comforted, because they are not.

But when Herod was dead, behold, an angel of the Lord appeareth in a dream to Joseph in Egypt, saying, Arise and take the young child and his mother, and go into the land of Israel: for they are dead that sought the young child's life. And he arose and took the young child and his mother, and came into the land of Israel. But when he heard that Archelaus was reigning over Judæa in the room of his father Herod, he was afraid to go thither; and being warned *of God* in a dream, he withdrew into the parts of Galilee, and came and dwelt in a city called Nazareth: that it might be fulfilled which was spoken by the prophets, that he should be called a Nazarene.[1]

[And when they had accomplished all things that were according to the law of the Lord, they returned into Galilee, to their own city Nazareth.][2]

---

1. Matt. 2: 13-23.   2. Luke 2: 39.

§9—THE CHILDHOOD OF JESUS.

And the child grew, and waxed strong, filled with wisdom: and the grace of God was upon him.

And his parents went every year to Jerusalem at the feast of the passover. And when he was twelve years old, they went up after the custom of the feast; and when they had fulfilled the days, as they were returning, the boy Jesus tarried behind in Jerusalem; and his parents knew it not; but supposing him to be in the company, they went a day's journey; and they sought for him among their kinsfolk and acquaintance: and when they found him not, they returned to Jerusalem, seeking for him. And it came to pass, after three days they found him in the temple, sitting in the midst of the doctors, both hearing them, and asking them questions: and all that heard him were amazed at his understanding and his answers. And when they saw him, they were astonished: and his mother said unto him, Son, why hast thou thus dealt with us? behold, thy father and I sought thee sorrowing. And he said unto them, How is it that ye sought me? wist ye not that I must be in my Father's house? And they understood not the saying which he spake unto them. And he went down with them, and came to Nazareth; and he was subject unto them: and his mother kept all *these* sayings in her heart.

And Jesus advanced in wisdom and stature, and in favour with God and men.[1]

§10—THE MINISTRY OF JOHN THE BAPTIST.

Now in the fifteenth year of the reign of Tiberius Cæsar, Pontius Pilate being governor of Judæa, and Herod being tetrarch of Galilee, and his brother Philip tetrarch of the region of Ituræa and Trachonitis, and Lysanias tetrarch of Abilene, in the high-priesthood of Annas and Caiaphas, the word of God came unto John the son of Zacharias in the wilderness. And he came into all the region round about Jordan, preaching the baptism of repentance unto remission

---

1. Luke 2: 40-52.

of sins,[1] saying, Repent ye; for the kingdom of heaven is at
hand.   For this is he that was spoken of by Isaiah the prophet, saying,[2]

Behold, I send my messenger before thy face,
Who shall prepare thy way;[3]
The voice of one crying in the wilderness,
Make ye ready the way of the Lord,
Make his paths straight.
Every valley shall be filled,
And every mountain and hill shall be brought low;
And the crooked shall become straight,
And the rough ways smooth;
And all flesh shall see the salvation of God.[4]

Now John himself had his raiment of camel's hair, and a
leathern girdle about his loins; and his food was locusts and
wild honey.   Then went out unto him Jerusalem, and all
Judæa, and all the region round about Jordan; and they
were baptized of him in the river Jordan, confessing their
sins.   But when he saw many of the Pharisees and Sadducees coming to his baptism, he said unto them, Ye offspring
of vipers, who warned you to flee from the wrath to come?
Bring forth therefore fruit worthy of repentance: and think
not to say within yourselves, We have Abraham to our
father: for I say unto you, that God is able of these stones
to raise up children unto Abraham.   And even now is the
axe laid unto the root of the trees: every tree therefore that
bringeth not forth good fruit is hewn down, and cast into
the fire.   I indeed baptize you with water unto repentance:
but he that cometh after me is mightier than I, whose shoes
I am not worthy to bear: he shall baptize you with the
Holy Ghost and *with* fire: whose fan is in his hand, and he
will throughly cleanse his threshing-floor; and he will gather
his wheat into the garner, but the chaff he will burn up with
unquenchable fire.[5]

And the multitude asked him, saying, What then must we
do?   And he answered and said unto them, He that hath

1. Luke 3: 1-4.   3. Mark 1: 2.   5. Matt. 3: 4-12.
2. Matt. 3: 2, 3.   4. Luke 3: 4-6.

two coats, let him impart to him that hath none; and he that hath food, let him do likewise. And there came also publicans to be baptized, and they said unto him, Master, what must we do? And he said unto them, Extort no more than that which is appointed you. And soldiers also asked him, saying, And we, what must we do? And he said unto them, Do violence to no man, neither exact *anything* wrongfully; and be content with your wages.

And as the people were in expectation, and all men reasoned in their hearts concerning John, whether haply he were the Christ; John answered, saying unto them all, I indeed baptize you with water; but there cometh he that is mightier than I, the latchet of whose shoes I am not worthy to unloose: he shall baptize you with the Holy Ghost and *with* fire: whose fan is in his hand, throughly to cleanse his threshing-floor, and to gather the wheat into his garner; but the chaff he will burn up with unquenchable fire.

With many other exhortations therefore preached he good tidings unto the people; but Herod the tetrarch, being reproved by him for Herodias his brother's wife, and for all the evil things which Herod had done, added yet this above all, that he shut up John in prison.[1]

§11—THE BAPTISM OF JESUS.

Then cometh Jesus from Galilee to the Jordan unto John, to be baptized of him. But John would have hindered him, saying, I have need to be baptized of thee, and comest thou to me? But Jesus answering said unto him, Suffer *it* now: for thus it becometh us to fulfil all righteousness. Then he suffereth him.[2]

Now it came to pass, when all the people were baptized, that, Jesus also having been baptized, and praying,[3] lo, the heavens were opened unto him, and he saw the Spirit of God descending as a dove, and coming upon him; and lo, a voice out of the heavens, saying, This is my beloved Son, in whom I am well pleased.[4]

---

1. Luke 3: 10-20.   3. Luke 3: 21.   4. Matt. 3: 16, 17.
2. Matt. 3: 13-15.

§ 12—THE TEMPTATION OF JESUS.

And Jesus, full of the Holy Spirit, returned from the Jordan, and was led by the Spirit in the wilderness during forty days, being tempted of the devil,[1] and he was with the wild beasts.[2] And he did eat nothing in those days : and when they were completed, he hungered. And the devil said unto him, If thou art the Son of God, command this stone that it become bread. And Jesus answered unto him, It is written, Man shall not live by bread alone,[3] but by every word that proceedeth out of the mouth of God. Then the devil taketh him into the holy city ; and he set him on the pinnacle of the temple, and saith unto him, If thou art the Son of God, cast thyself down : for it is written,

He shall give his angels charge concerning thee[4] (to guard thee[5]):
And on their hands they shall bear thee up,
Lest haply thou dash thy foot against a stone.

Jesus said unto him, Again it is written, Thou shalt not tempt the Lord thy God. Again the devil taketh him unto an exceeding high mountain, and sheweth him all the kingdoms of the world, and the glory of them,[6] in a moment of time. And the devil said unto him, To thee will I give all this authority, and the glory of them : for it hath been delivered unto me ; and to whomsoever I will I give it. If thou therefore wilt worship before me, it shall all be thine.[7] Then saith Jesus unto him, Get thee hence, Satan : for it is written, Thou shalt worship the Lord thy God, and him only shalt thou serve.[8] And when the devil had completed every temptation, he departed from him for a season ;[9] and behold, angels came and ministered unto him.[10]

1. Luke 4 : 1, 2.
2. Mark 1 : 13.
3. Luke 4 : 2-4.
4. Matt. 4 : 4-6.
5. Luke 4 : 13.
6. Matt. 4 : 6-8.
7. Luke 4 : 5-7.
8. Matt. 4 : 10.
9. Luke 4 : 13.
10. Matt. 4 : 11.

§ 13—JOHN'S TESTIMONY CONCERNING JESUS.

And this is the witness of John, when the Jews sent unto him from Jerusalem priests and Levites to ask him, Who art thou? And he confessed, and denied not; and he confessed, I am not the Christ. And they asked him, What then? Art thou Elijah? And he saith, I am not. Art thou the prophet? And he answered, No. They said therefore unto him, Who art thou? that we may give an answer to them that sent us. What sayest thou of thyself? He said, I am the voice of one crying in the wilderness, Make straight the way of the Lord, as said Isaiah the prophet. And they had been sent from the Pharisees. And they asked him, and said unto him, Why then baptizest thou, if thou art not the Christ, neither Elijah, neither the prophet? John answered them, saying, I baptize with water: in the midst of you standeth one whom ye know not, *even* he that cometh after me, the latchet of whose shoe I am not worthy to unloose. These things were done in Bethany beyond Jordan, where John was baptizing.

On the morrow he seeth Jesus coming unto him, and saith, Behold, the Lamb of God, which taketh away the sin of the world! This is he of whom I said, After me cometh a man which is become before me: for he was before me. And I knew him not; but that he should be made manifest to Israel, for this cause came I baptizing with water. And John bare witness, saying, I have beheld the Spirit descending as a dove out of heaven; and it abode upon him. And I knew him not: but he that sent me to baptize with water, he said unto me, Upon whomsoever thou shalt see the Spirit descending, and abiding upon him, the same is he that baptizeth with the Holy Spirit. And I have seen, and have borne witness that this is the Son of God.

Again on the morrow John was standing, and two of his disciples; and he looked upon Jesus as he walked, and saith, Behold, the Lamb of God! And the two disciples heard him speak, and they followed Jesus.[1] And Jesus turned, and

---

1. John 1: 19-37.

beheld them following, and saith unto them, What seek ye ? And they said unto him, Rabbi (which is to say, being interpreted, Master), where abidest thou ? He saith unto them, Come, and ye shall see. They came therefore and saw where he abode ; and they abode with him that day : it was about the tenth hour.[1]

§ 14—THE CALL OF THE FIRST DISCIPLES.

And Jesus himself, when he began *to teach*, was about thirty years of age.[2]

One of the two that heard John *speak*, and followed him, was Andrew, Simon Peter's brother. He findeth first his own brother Simon, and saith unto him, We have found the Messiah (which is, being interpreted, Christ). He brought him unto Jesus. Jesus looked upon him, and said, Thou art Simon the son of John : thou shalt be called Cephas (which is by interpretation, Peter).

On the morrow he was minded to go forth into Galilee, and he findeth Philip : and Jesus saith unto him, Follow me. Now Philip was from Bethsaida, of the city of Andrew and Peter. Philip findeth Nathanael, and saith unto him, We have found him, of whom Moses in the law, and the prophets, did write, Jesus of Nazareth, the son of Joseph. And Nathanael said unto him, Can any good thing come out of Nazareth ? Philip saith unto him, Come and see. Jesus saw Nathanael coming to him, and saith of him, Behold, an Israelite indeed, in whom is no guile ! Nathanael saith unto him, Whence knowest thou me ? Jesus answered and said unto him, Before Philip called thee, when thou wast under the fig tree, I saw thee. Nathanael answered him, Rabbi, thou art the Son of God ; thou art King of Israel. Jesus answered and said unto him, Because I said unto thee, I saw thee underneath the fig tree, believest thou ? thou shalt see greater things than these. And he saith unto him, Verily, verily, I say unto you, Ye shall see the heaven opened, and the angels of God ascending and descending upon the Son of man.[3]

---

1. John 1 : 38-39.   2. Luke 3 : 23.   3. John 1 : 40-51.

§ 15—THE FIRST MIRACLE OF JESUS.

And the third day there was a marriage in Cana of Galilee ; and the mother of Jesus was there : and Jesus also was bidden, and his disciples, to the marriage. And when the wine failed, the mother of Jesus saith unto him, They have no wine. And Jesus saith unto her, Woman, what have I to do with thee ? mine hour is not yet come. His mother saith unto the servants, Whatsoever he saith unto you, do it. Now there were six waterpots of stone set there after the Jews' manner of purifying, containing two or three firkins apiece. Jesus saith unto them, Fill the waterpots with water. And they filled them up to the brim. And he saith unto them, Draw out now, and bear unto the ruler of the feast. And they bare it. And when the ruler of the feast tasted the water now become wine, and knew not whence it was (but the servants which had drawn the water knew), the ruler of the feast calleth the bridegroom, and saith unto him, Every man setteth on first the good wine ; and when *men* have drunk freely, *then* that which is worse : thou hast kept the good wine until now. This beginning of his signs did Jesus in Cana of Galilee, and manifested his glory ; and his disciples believed on him.

After this he went down to Capernaum, he, and his mother, and *his* brethren, and his disciples : and there they abode not many days.[1]

§ 16—JESUS PURGES THE TEMPLE (THE FIRST TIME).

And the passover of the Jews was at hand, and Jesus went up to Jerusalem. And he found in the temple those that sold oxen and sheep and doves, and the changers of money sitting : and he made a scourge of cords, and cast all out of the temple, both the sheep and the oxen ; and he poured out the changers' money, and overthrew their tables ; and to them that sold the doves he said, Take these things hence ; make not my Father's house a house of merchandise.

---

1. John 2: 1-12.

His disciples remembered that it was written, The zeal of
thine house shall eat me up.   The Jews therefore answered
and said unto him, What sign shewest thou unto us, seeing
that thou doest these things?   Jesus answered and said unto
them, Destroy this temple, and in three days I will raise it
up.   The Jews therefore said, Forty and six years was this
temple in building, and wilt thou raise it up in three days?
But he spake of the temple of his body.   When therefore
he was raised from the dead, his disciples remembered that
he spake this ; and they believed the scripture, and the
word which Jesus had said.

Now when he was in Jerusalem at the passover, during
the feast, many believed on his name, beholding his signs
which he did.   But Jesus did not trust himself unto them,
for that he knew all men, and because he needed not that
any one should bear witness concerning man ; for he himself
knew what was in man.[1]

§ 17—THE DISCOURSE OF JESUS WITH NICODEMUS.

Now there was a man of the Pharisees, named Nicodemus, a
ruler of the Jews : the same came unto him by night, and
said to him, Rabbi, we know that thou art a teacher come
from God : for no man can do these signs that thou doest,
except God be with him.   Jesus answered and said unto
him, Verily, verily, I say unto thee, Except a man be born
anew, he cannot see the kingdom of God.   Nicodemus saith
unto him, How can a man be born when he is old ? can he
enter a second time into his mother's womb, and be born?
Jesus answered, Verily, verily, I say unto thee, Except a
man be born of water and the Spirit, he cannot enter into
the kingdom of God.   That which is born of the flesh is
flesh ; and that which is born of the Spirit is spirit.   Marvel
not that I said unto thee, Ye must be born anew.   The wind
bloweth where it listeth, and thou hearest the voice thereof,
but knowest not whence it cometh, and whither it goeth :
so is every one that is born of the Spirit.   Nicodemus

---

1. John 2 : 13-25.

answered and said unto him, How can these things be?
Jesus answered and said unto him, Art thou the teacher of
Israel, and understandest not these things? Verily, verily,
I say unto thee, We speak that we do know, and bear witness of that we have seen ; and ye receive not our witness.
If I told you earthly things, and ye believe not, how shall
ye believe, if I tell you heavenly things? And no man hath
ascended into heaven, but he that descended out of heaven,
even the Son of man, which is in heaven. And as Moses
lifted up the serpent in the wilderness, even so must the
Son of man be lifted up : that whosoever believeth may in
him have eternal life.

For God so loved the world, that he gave his only
begotten Son, that whosoever believeth on him should not
perish, but have eternal life. For God sent not the Son
into the world to judge the world ; but that the world
should be saved through him. He that believeth on him is
not judged : he that believeth not hath been judged already,
because he hath not believed on the name of the only
begotten Son of God. And this is the judgement, that the
light is come into the world, and men loved the darkness
rather than the light; for their works were evil. For every
one that doeth ill hateth the light, and cometh not to the
light, lest his works should be reproved. But he that doeth
the truth cometh to the light, that his works may be made
manifest, that they have been wrought in God.[1]

§ 18—JOHN THE BAPTIST'S LAST TESTIMONY TO JESUS. JOHN'S IMPRISONMENT.

After these things came Jesus and his disciples into the
land of Judæa; and there he tarried with them, and baptized. And John also was baptizing in Ænon near to Salim,
because there was much water there : and they came, and
were baptized. For John was not yet cast into prison.
There arose therefore a questioning on the part of John's
disciples with a Jew about purifying. And they came unto

---

1. John 3 : 1-21.

John, and said to him, Rabbi, he that was with thee beyond Jordan, to whom thou hast borne witness, behold, the same baptizeth, and all men come to him. John answered and said, A man can receive nothing, except it have been given him from heaven. Ye yourselves bear me witness, that I said, I am not the Christ, but, that I am sent before him. He that hath the bride is the bridegroom : but the friend of the bridegroom, which standeth and heareth him, rejoiceth greatly because of the bridegroom's voice : this my joy therefore is fulfilled. He must increase, but I must decrease.

He that cometh from above is above all : he that is of the earth is of the earth, and of the earth he speaketh : he that cometh from heaven is above all. What he hath seen and heard, of that he beareth witness ; and no man receiveth his witness. He that hath received his witness hath set his seal to *this*, that God is true. For he whom God hath sent speaketh the words of God : for he giveth not the Spirit by measure. The Father loveth the Son, and hath given all things into his hand. He that believeth on the Son hath eternal life ; but he that obeyeth not the Son shall not see life, but the wrath of God abideth on him.[1]

When therefore the Lord knew how that the Pharisees had heard that Jesus was making and baptizing more dis- ciples than John (although Jesus himself baptized not, but his disciples), he left Judæa, and departed again into Gal- ilee.[2] For Herod himself had sent forth and laid hold upon John, and bound him in prison for the sake of Herodias, his brother Philip's wife : for he had married her. For John said unto Herod, It is not lawful for thee to have thy brother's wife. And Herodias set herself against him, and desired to kill him ; and she could not ; for Herod feared John, knowing that he was a righteous man and a holy, and kept him safe ;[3] [and] he feared the multitude because they counted him as a prophet.[4] And when he heard him, he was much perplexed ; and he heard him gladly.[5]

---

1. John 3 : 22-36.   3. Mark 6 : 17-20.   5. Mark 6 : 20.
2. John 4 : 1-3.   4. Matt. 14 : 5.

§ 19—JESUS TEACHES THE WOMAN OF SAMARIA.

And he [Jesus] must needs pass through Samaria. So he cometh to a city of Samaria, called Sychar, near to the parcel of ground that Jacob gave to his son Joseph : and Jacob's well was there. Jesus therefore, being wearied with his journey, sat thus by the well. It was about the sixth hour. There cometh a woman of Samaria to draw water : Jesus saith unto her, Give me to drink. For his disciples were gone away into the city to buy food. The Samaritan woman therefore saith unto him, How is it that thou, being a Jew, askest drink of me, which am a Samaritan woman? (For Jews have no dealings with Samaritans.) Jesus answered and said unto her. If thou knewest the gift of God, and who it is that saith to thee, Give me to drink ; thou wouldest have asked of him, and he would have given thee living water. The woman saith unto him, Sir, thou hast nothing to draw with, and the well is deep : from whence then hast thou that living water? Art thou greater than our father Jacob, which gave us the well, and drank thereof himself, and his sons, and his cattle? Jesus answered and said unto her, Every one that drinketh of this water shall thirst again : but whosoever drinketh of the water that I shall give him shall never thirst ; but the water that I shall give him shall become in him a well of water springing up unto eternal life. The woman saith unto him, Sir, give me this water, that I thirst not, neither come all the way hither to draw. Jesus saith unto her, Go, call thy husband, and come hither. The woman answered and said unto him, I have no husband. Jesus saith unto her, Thou saidst well, I have no husband : for thou hast had five husbands ; and he whom thou now hast is not thy husband : this hast thou said truly. The woman saith unto him, Sir, I perceive that thou art a prophet. Our fathers worshipped in this mountain ; and ye say, that in Jerusalem is the place where men ought to worship. Jesus saith unto her, Woman, believe me, the hour cometh, when neither in this mountain, nor in Jerusalem, shall ye worship the Father.[1] Ye worship that which ye

---

1. John 4 : 4-21.

know not : we worship that which we know : for salvation is from the Jews. But the hour cometh, and now is, when the true worshippers shall worship the Father in spirit and truth : for such doth the father seek to be his worshippers. God is a Spirit : and they that worship him must worship in spirit and truth. The woman saith unto him, I know that Messiah cometh (which is called Christ): when he is come, he will declare unto us all things. Jesus saith unto her, I that speak unto thee am *he.*

And upon this came his disciples ; and they marvelled that he was speaking with a woman ; yet no man said, What seekest thou? or, Why speakest thou with her? So the woman left her waterpot, and went away into the city. and saith to the men, Come, see a man, which told me all things that *ever* I did : can this be the Christ? They went out of the city, and were coming to him. In the meanwhile the disciples prayed him, saying, Rabbi, eat. But he said unto them, I have meat to eat that ye know not. The disciples therefore said one to another, Hath any man brought him *aught* to eat? Jesus saith unto them, My meat is to do the will of him that sent me. and to accomplish his work. Say not ye, There are yet four months, and *then* cometh the harvest? behold, I say unto you, Lift up your eyes, and look on the fields, that they are white already unto harvest. He that reapeth receiveth wages, and gathereth fruit unto life eternal ; that he that soweth and he that reapeth may rejoice together. For herein is the saying true, One soweth, and another reapeth. I sent you to reap that whereon ye have not laboured : others have laboured, and ye are entered into their labour.

And from that city many of the Samaritans believed on him because of the word of the woman, who testified, He told me all things that *ever* I did. So when the Samaritans came unto him, they besought him to abide with them: and he abode there two days. And many more believed because of his word ; and they said to the woman, Now we believe, not because of thy speaking : for we have heard for ourselves, and know that this is indeed the Saviour of the world.[1]

---

1. John 4 : 22-42.

§ 20—JESUS HEALS A NOBLEMAN'S SON.

And after the two days[1] Jesus returned in the power of the Spirit into Galilee.[2] For Jesus himself testified, that a prophet hath no honour in his own country.[3] And a fame went out concerning him through all the region round about. And he taught in the synagogues, being glorified of all.[4] So when he came into Galilee, the Galilæans received him, having seen all the things that he did in Jerusalem at the feast: for they also went unto the feast.

He came therefore again unto Cana of Galilee, where he made the water wine. And there was a certain nobleman, whose son was sick at Capernaum. When he heard that Jesus was come out of Judæa into Galilee, he went unto him, and besought *him* that he would come down, and heal his son ; for he was at the point of death. Jesus therefore said unto him, Except ye see signs and wonders, ye will in no wise believe. The nobleman saith unto him, Sir, come down ere my child die. Jesus saith unto him, Go thy way; thy son liveth. The man believed the word that Jesus spake unto him, and he went his way. And as he was now going down, his servants met him, saying, that his son lived. So he inquired of them the hour when he began to amend. They said therefore unto him, Yesterday at the seventh hour the fever left him. So the father knew that *it was* at that hour in which Jesus said unto him, Thy son liveth : and himself believed, and his whole house. This is again the second sign that Jesus did, having come out of Judæa into Galilee.[5]

§21—JESUS IS REJECTED AT NAZARETH.

And he came to Nazareth, where he had been brought up : and he entered, as his custom was, into the synagogue on the sabbath day, and stood up to read. And there was delivered unto him the book of the prophet Isaiah. And

---

1. John 4 : 43.   3. John 4 : 44.   5. John 4 : 45-54.
2. Luke 4 : 14.   4. Luke 4 : 14, 15.

he opened the book, and found the place where it was written,

> The Spirit of the Lord is upon me,
> Because he anointed me to preach good tidings to the
>   poor :
> He hath sent me to proclaim release to the captives,
> And recovering of sight to the blind,
> To set at liberty them that are bruised,
> To proclaim the acceptable year of the Lord.

And he closed the book, and gave it back to the attendant, and sat down : and the eyes of all in the synagogue were fastened on him. And he began to say unto them, To-day hath this scripture been fulfilled in your ears. And all bare him witness, and wondered at the words of grace which proceeded out of his mouth : and they said, Is not this Joseph's son ? And he said unto them, Doubtless ye will say unto me this parable, Physician, heal thyself : whatsoever we have heard done at Capernaum, do also here in thine own country. And he said, Verily I say unto you, No prophet is acceptable in his own country. But of a truth I say unto you, There were many widows in Israel in the days of Elijah, when the heaven was shut up three years and six months, when there came a great famine over all the land ; and unto none of them was Elijah sent, but only to Zarephath, in the land of Sidon, unto a woman that was a widow. And there were many lepers in Israel in the time of Elisha the prophet ; and none of them was cleansed, but only Naaman the Syrian. And they were all filled with wrath in the synagogue, as they heard these things ; and they rose up, and cast him forth out of the city, and led him unto the brow of the hill whereon their city was built, that they might throw him down headlong. But he passing through the midst of them went his way.[1]

---

1. Luke 4 : 16-30.

§ 22—THE CALL OF PETER, JAMES AND JOHN.

And leaving Nazareth, [Jesus] came and dwelt in Caper-
naum, which is by the sea, in the borders of Zebulun and
Naphtali : that it might be fulfilled which was spoken by
Isaiah the prophet, saying,
>The land of Zebulun and the land of Naphtali,
>Toward the sea, beyond Jordan,
>Galilee of the Gentiles,
>The people which sat in darkness
>Saw a great light,
>And to them which sat in the region and shadow of
>   death,
>To them did light spring up.

From that time began Jesus to preach[1] the gospel of God,
saying, The time is fulfilled, and the kingdom of God is at
hand : repent ye, and believe in the gospel.[2]

And walking by the sea of Galilee, he saw two brethren,
Simon who is called Peter, and Andrew his brother, casting
a net into the sea ; for they were fishers. And he saith
unto them, Come ye after me, and I will make you fishers
of men. And they straightway left the nets, and followed
him. And going on from thence he saw other two brethren,
James the *son* of Zebedee, and John his brother, in the
boat with Zebedee their father, mending their nets.[3] And
straightway he called them : and they left their father
Zebedee in the boat with the hired servants, and went after
him.[4]

§ 23—JESUS HEALS A DEMONIAC, AND OTHERS.

And they go into Capernaum ; and straightway on the
sabbath day he entered into the synagogue and taught. And
they were astonished at his teaching : for he taught them as
having authority, and not as the scribes. And straightway
there was in their synagogue a man with an unclean spirit ;
and he cried out,[5] with a loud voice,[6] saying, What have we

---

1. Matt. 4 : 13-17.   3. Matt. 4 : 18-21.   5. Mark 1 : 21-24.
2. Mark 1 : 14, 15.   4. Mark 1 : 20.   6. Luke 4 : 34.

to do with thee, thou Jesus of Nazareth? art thou come to destroy us? I know thee who thou art, the Holy One of God. And Jesus rebuked him, saying, Hold thy peace, and come out of him. And the unclean spirit, tearing him and crying with a loud voice, came out of him,[1] having done him no hurt.[2] And they were all amazed, insomuch that they questioned among themselves, saying. What is this? a new teaching! with authority he commandeth even the unclean spirits, and they obey him. And the report of him went out straightway everywhere into all the region of Galilee round about.

And straightway, when they were come out of the synagogue, they came into the house of Simon and Andrew, with James and John. Now Simon's wife's mother lay sick of a fever; and straightway they tell him of her: and he came[3] and stood over her, and rebuked the fever,[4] and took her by the hand, and raised her up; and the fever left her, and she ministered unto them.[5]

And when the sun was setting, all they that had any sick with divers diseases brought them unto him; and he laid his hands on every one of them, and healed them,[6] that it might be fulfilled which was spoken by Isaiah the prophet, saying. Himself took our infirmities, and bare our diseases.[7] And all the city was gathered together at the door. And he healed many that were sick with divers diseases.[8] And devils also came out from many, crying out, and saying, Thou art the Son of God. And rebuking them, he suffered them not to speak, because they knew that he was the Christ.[9]

And in the morning, a great while before day, he rose up and went out, and departed into a desert place, and there prayed. And Simon and they that were with him followed after him; and they found him, and say unto him, All are seeking thee. And he saith unto them, Let us go elsewhere into the next towns, that I may preach there also; for to

---

1. Mark 1: 24-27.
2. Luke 4: 35.
3. Mark 1: 26-30.

4. Luke 4: 39.
5. Mark 1: 30, 31.
6. Luke 4: 40.

7. Matt. 8: 17.
8. Mark 1: 33, 34.
9. Luke 4: 41.

this end came I forth. And he went into their synagogues throughout all Galilee,[1] teaching in their synagogues, and preaching the gospel of the kingdom, and healing all manner of disease and all manner of sickness among the people. And the report of him went forth into all Syria : and they brought unto him all that were sick, holden with divers diseases and torments, possessed with devils, and epileptic, and palsied ; and he healed them. And there followed him great multitudes from Galilee and Decapolis and Jerusalem and Judæa and *from* beyond Jordan.[2]

§24—THE MIRACULOUS DRAUGHT OF FISHES.

Now it came to pass while the multitude pressed upon him and heard the word of God, that he was standing by the lake of Gennesaret ; and he saw two boats standing by the lake : but the fishermen had gone out of them, and were washing their nets. And he entered into one of the boats, which was Simon's, and asked him to put out a little from the land. And he sat down and taught the multitudes out of the boat. And when he had left speaking, he said unto Simon, Put out into the deep, and let down your nets for a draught. And Simon answered and said, Master, we toiled all night, and took nothing: but at thy word I will let down the nets. And when they had this done, they inclosed a great multitude of fishes ; and their nets were breaking ; and they beckoned unto their partners in the other boat, that they should come and help them. And they came, and filled both the boats, so that they began to sink. But Simon Peter, when he saw it, fell down at Jesus' knees, saying, Depart from me ; for I am a sinful man, O Lord. For he was amazed, and all that were with him, at the draught of the fishes which they had taken : and so were also James and John, sons of Zebedee, which were partners with Simon. And Jesus said unto Simon, Fear not ; from henceforth thou shalt catch men. And when they had brought their boats to land, they left all, and followed him.[3]

---

1. Mark 1 : 35-39.   2. Matt. 4 : 23-25.   3. Luke 5 : 1-11.

§25—JESUS HEALS A LEPER AND A PARALYTIC.

And it came to pass, while he was in one of the cities, behold, a man full of leprosy : and when he saw Jesus, he fell on his face, and besought him, saying, Lord, if thou wilt, thou canst make me clean. And[1] being moved with compassion,[2] he stretched forth his hand, and touched him, saying, I will ; be thou made clean. And straightway the leprosy departed from him,[3] and he was made clean. And he strictly charged him, and straightway sent him out, and saith unto him, See thou say nothing to any man : but go thy way, shew thyself to the priest, and offer for thy cleansing the things which Moses commanded, for a testimony unto them. But he went out, and began to publish it much, and to spread abroad the matter,[4] and great multitudes came together to hear, and to be healed of their infirmities,[5] insomuch that Jesus could no more openly enter into a city, but was without in desert places : and they came to him from every quarter.[6]

And he entered into a boat, and crossed over, and came into his own city.[7] And when he entered again into Capernaum after some days, it was noised that he was in the house.[8]

And it came to pass on one of those days that he was teaching ; and there were Pharisees and doctors of the law sitting by, which were come out of every village of Galilee and Judæa and Jerusalem : and the power of the Lord was with him to heal.[9] And many were gathered together, so that there was no longer room *for them*, no, not even about the door.[10] And behold, men bring on a bed a man that was palsied : and they sought to bring him in, and to lay him before him. And not finding by what *way* they might bring him in because of the multitude, they went up to the housetop, and[11] uncovered the roof where he was : and when they had broken it up, they[12] let him down through the tiles

---

1. Luke 5 : 12.	5. Luke 5 : 15.	9 Luke 5 : 17.
2. Mark 1 : 41.	6. Mark 1 : 45.	10. Mark 2 : 2.
3. Luke 5 : 13.	7. Matt. 9 : 1.	11. Luke 5 : 18, 19.
4. Mark 1 : 43-45.	8. Mark 2 : 1.	12. Mark 2 : 5.

with his couch into the midst before Jesus.[1] And Jesus seeing their faith saith unto the sick of the palsy, Son, thy sins are forgiven. But there were certain of the scribes sitting there, and reasoning in their hearts, Why doth this man thus speak? he blasphemeth : who can forgive sins but one, even God? And straightway Jesus, perceiving in his spirit that they so reasoned within themselves, saith unto them, Why reason ye these things in your hearts? Whether is easier, to say to the sick of the palsy, Thy sins are forgiven ; or to say, Arise, and take up thy bed, and walk? But that ye may know that the Son of man hath power on earth to forgive sins (he saith to the sick of the palsy), I say unto thee, Arise, take up thy bed, and go unto thy house. And he arose, and straightway took up the bed, and went forth before them all[2] to his house, glorifying God. And amazement took hold on all, and they glorified God,[3] which had given such power unto men ;[4] and they were filled with fear, saying, We have seen strange things to-day.[5]

§ 26—THE CALL OF MATTHEW AND DISCOURSE AT HIS HOUSE.

And as Jesus passed by from thence,[6] he went forth again by the sea side ; and all the multitude resorted unto him, and he taught them. And as he passed by, he saw[7] a publican named[8] Levi the son of Alphæus sitting at the place of toll, and he saith unto him, Follow me.[9] And he forsook all, and rose up and followed him. And Levi made him a great feast.[10] And it came to pass, that he was sitting at meat in his house, and many publicans and sinners sat down with Jesus and his disciples : for there were many, and they followed him. And the scribes of the Pharisees, when they saw that he was eating with the sinners and publicans, said unto his disciples, He eateth and drinketh with publicans and sinners. And when Jesus heard it, he saith

1. Luke 5 : 19.
2. Mark 2 : 5-12.
3. Luke 5 : 25, 26.
4. Matt. 9 : 8.
5. Luke 5 : 26.
6. Matt. 9 : 9.
7. Mark 2 : 13, 14.
8. Luke 5 : 27.
9. Mark 2 : 14, 15.
10. Luke 5 : 28, 29.

unto them, They that are whole have no need of a physician, but they that are sick.[1] But go ye and learn what *this* meaneth, I desire mercy, and not sacrifice : for I came not to call the righteous, but sinners.[2]

And John's disciples and the Pharisees were fasting : and they come and say unto him,[3] The disciples of John fast often, and make supplications ; likewise also the *disciples* of the Pharisees,[4] but thy disciples fast not. And Jesus said unto them, Can the sons of the bride-chamber fast, while the bridegroom is with them? as long as they have the bridegroom with them, they cannot fast. But the days will come, when the bridegroom shall be taken away from them, and then will they fast in that day.[5] And he spake also a parable unto them ; No man rendeth a piece from a new garment and putteth it upon an old garment ; else he will rend the new, and also the piece from the new will not agree with the old,[6] and a worse rent is made.[7] And no man putteth new wine into old wine-skins ; else the new wine will burst the skins, and itself will be spilled, and the skins will perish. But new wine must be put into fresh wine-skins[8] and both are preserved.[9] And no man having drunk old *wine* desireth new : for he saith, The old is good.[10]

§ 27—THE TEACHING OF JESUS CONCERNING THE SABBATH.

At that season Jesus went on the sabbath day through the cornfields ; and his disciples were an hungred, and began to pluck ears of corn, and to eat. But[11] certain of[12] the Pharisees, when they saw it, said unto him, Behold, thy disciples do that which it is not lawful to do upon the sabbath. But he said unto them, Have ye not read what David did, when he was an hungred, and they that were

---

1. Mark 2 : 15-17.
2. Matt. 9 : 13.
3. Mark 2 : 18.
4. Luke 5 : 33.
5. Mark 2 : 18-20.
6. Luke 5 : 36.
7. Mark 2 : 21.
8. Luke 5 : 37, 38.
9. Matt. 9 : 17.
10. Luke 5 : 39.
11. Matt. 12 : 1.
12. Luke 6 : 2.

with him ; how he entered into the house of God[1] when Abiathar was high priest, and did eat the shewbread, which it is not lawful to eat save for the priests[2] [alone[3]], and gave also to them that were with him?[4]   Or have ye not read in the law, how that on the sabbath day the priests in the temple profane the sabbath. and are guiltless? But I say unto you, that one greater than the temple is here.   But if ye had known what this meaneth, I desire mercy, and not sacrifice, ye would not have condemned the guiltless.[5]   And he said unto them, The sabbath was made for man, and not man for the sabbath : so that the Son of man is lord even of the sabbath.[6]

And he departed thence, and[7] it came to pass on another sabbath, that he entered into the synagogue and taught : and there was a man there, and his right hand was withered. And the scribes and the Pharisees watched him, whether he would heal on the sabbath; that they might find how to accuse him.   But he knew their thoughts ; and he said to the man that had his hand withered, Rise up, and stand forth in the midst.   And he arose and stood forth.   And Jesus said unto them, I ask you, Is it lawful on the sabbath to do good, or to do harm? to save a life, or to destroy it ?[8]   And he said unto them, What man shall there be of you, that shall have one sheep, and if this fall into a pit on the sabbath day, will he not lay hold on it, and lift it out? How much then is a man of more value than a sheep! Wherefore it is lawful to do good on the sabbath day.[9]   But they held their peace.   And when he had looked round about on them with anger, being grieved at the hardening of their heart, he saith unto the man, Stretch forth thy hand.   And he stretched it forth : and his hand was restored.[10]   But they were filled with madness ; and communed one with another what they might do to Jesus.[11]   And the Pharisees went out, and straightway with the Herodians took counsel against him, how they might destroy him.[12]

---

1. Matt. 12 : 2-4.   5. Matt. 12 : 5-7.   9. Matt. 12 : 11, 12.
2. Mark 2 : 26.   6. Mark 2 : 27, 28.   10. Mark 3 : 5.
3. Luke 6 : 4.   7. Matt. 12 : 9.   11. Luke 6 : 2.
4. Mark 2 : 26.   8. Luke 6 : 6-9.   12. Mark 3 : 6.

§ 28—JESUS HEALS A SICK MAN AT THE POOL OF BETHESDA.

After these things there was a feast of the Jews ; and Jesus went up to Jerusalem.

Now there is in Jerusalem by the sheep *gate* a pool, which is called in Hebrew Bethesda, having five porches. In these lay a multitude of them that were sick, blind, halt, withered. And a certain man was there, which had been thirty and eight years in his infirmity. When Jesus saw him lying, and knew that he had been now a long time *in that case*, he saith unto him, Wouldest thou be made whole ? The sick man answered him, Sir, I have no man, when the water is troubled, to put me into the pool : but while I am coming, another steppeth down before me. Jesus saith unto him, Arise, take up thy bed, and walk. And straightway the man was made whole, and took up his bed and walked.

Now it was the sabbath on that day. So the Jews said unto him that was cured, It is the sabbath, and it is not lawful for thee to take up thy bed. But he answered them, He that made me whole, the same said unto me, Take up thy bed, and walk. They asked him, Who is the man that said unto thee, Take up *thy bed*, and walk ? But he that was healed wist not who it was : for Jesus had conveyed himself away, a multitude being in the place. Afterward Jesus findeth him in the temple, and said unto him, Behold, thou art made whole : sin no more, lest a worse thing befall thee. The man went away, and told the Jews that it was Jesus which had made him whole. And for this cause did the Jews persecute Jesus, because he did these things on the sabbath. But Jesus answered them, My Father worketh even until now, and I work. For this cause therefore the Jews sought the more to kill him, because he not only brake the sabbath, but also called God his own Father, making himself equal with God.[1]

---

1. John 5 : 1-18.

§ 29—JESUS REPROVES THE PERSECUTING JEWS.

Jesus therefore answered and said unto them,

Verily, verily, I say unto you, The Son can do nothing of himself, but what he seeth the Father doing : for what things soever he doeth, these the Son also doeth in like manner. For the Father loveth the Son, and sheweth him all things that himself doeth : and greater works than these will he shew him, that ye may marvel. For as the Father raiseth the dead and quickeneth them, even so the Son also quickeneth whom he will. For neither doth the Father judge any man, but he hath given all judgement unto the Son ; that all may honour the Son, even as they honour the Father. He that honoureth not the Son honoureth not the Father which sent him. Verily, verily, I say unto you, He that heareth my word, and believeth him that sent me, hath eternal life, and cometh not into judgement, but hath passed out of death into life. Verily, verily, I say unto you, The hour cometh, and now is, when the dead shall hear the voice of the Son of God ; and they that hear shall live. For as the Father hath life in himself, even so gave he to the Son also to have life in himself : and he gave him authority to execute judgement, because he is the Son of man. Marvel not at this : for the hour cometh, in which all that are in the tombs shall hear his voice, and shall come forth ; they that have done good, unto the resurrection of life ; and they that have done ill, unto the resurrection of judgement.

I can of myself do nothing : as I hear, I judge : and my judgement is righteous ; because I seek not mine own will, but the will of him that sent me. If I bear witness of myself, my witness is not true. It is another that beareth witness of me ; and I know that the witness which he witnesseth of me is true. Ye have sent unto John, and he hath borne witness unto the truth. But the witness which I receive is not from man : howbeit I say these things, that ye may be saved. He was the lamp that burneth and shineth : and ye were willing to rejoice for a season in his[1]

---

1. John 5 : 19-35.

light.   But the witness which I have is greater than *that of*
John : for the works which the Father hath given me to
accomplish, the very works that I do, bear witness of me,
that the Father hath sent me.   And the Father which sent
me, he hath borne witness of me.   Ye have neither heard
his voice at any time, nor seen his form.   And ye have
not his word abiding in you : for whom he sent, him ye
believe not.   Ye search the scriptures, because ye think
that in them ye have eternal life ; and these are they
which bear witness of me ; and ye will not come to me,
that ye may have life.   I receive not glory from men.
But I know you, that ye have not the love of God in yourselves.   I am come in my Father's name, and ye receive
me not : if another shall come in his own name, him ye
will receive.   How can ye believe, which receive glory one
of another, and the glory that *cometh* from the only God
ye seek not?   Think not that I will accuse you to the
Father : there is one that accuseth you, *even* Moses, on
whom ye have set your hope.   For if ye believed Moses, ye
would believe me ; for he wrote of me.   But if ye believe
not his writings, how shall ye believe my words ?[1]

§30—JESUS WORKS MANY MIRACLES BY
THE SEA SIDE.

And Jesus with his disciples withdrew to the sea : and a
great multitude from Galilee followed : and from Judæa, and
from Jerusalem, and from Idumæa, and beyond Jordan, and
about Tyre and Sidon, a great multitude, hearing what great
things he did, came unto him.   And he spake to his disciples,
that a little boat should wait on him because of the crowd,
lest they should throng him : for he had healed many ; insomuch that as many as had plagues pressed upon him that
they might touch him.   And the unclean spirits, whensoever
they beheld him, fell down before him, and cried, saying,
Thou art the Son of God.   And he charged them much
that they should not make him known,[2] that it might be
fulfilled which was spoken by Isaiah the prophet, saying,

---

1. John 5 : 36-47.   2. Mark 3 : 7-12.

Behold, my servant whom I have chosen ;
My beloved in whom my soul is well pleased :
I will put my Spirit upon him,
And he shall declare judgement to the Gentiles.
He shall not strive, nor cry aloud ;
Neither shall any one hear his voice in the streets.
A bruised reed shall he not break,
And smoking flax shall he not quench,
Till he send forth judgement unto victory.
And in his name shall the Gentiles hope.[1]

§31—THE CALL OF THE TWELVE APOSTLES.

And it came to pass in these days, that he went out into the mountain to pray; and he continued all night in prayer to God. And when it was day, he called[2] unto him whom he himself would : and they went unto him. And he appointed twelve,[3] whom also he named apostles,[4] that they might be with him, and that he might send them forth to preach, and to have authority[5] over unclean spirits, to cast them out, and to heal all manner of disease and all manner of sickness,[6] [and] to cast out devils : and Simon he surnamed Peter ; and James the *son* of Zebedee, and John the brother of James ; and them he surnamed Boanerges, which is, Sons of thunder : and Andrew, and Philip, and Bartholomew, and Matthew, and Thomas, and James the *son* of Alphæus, and Thaddæus, and Simon the Cananæan,[7] which was called the Zealot, and Judas *the son* of James, and Judas Iscariot, which was the traitor,[8] which also betrayed him.[9] And he came down with them, and stood on a level place, and a great multitude of his disciples, and a great number of the people from all Judæa and Jerusalem, and the sea coast of Tyre and Sidon, which came to hear him, and to be healed of their diseases ; and they that were troubled with unclean spirits were healed. And all the multitude sought to touch him : for power came forth from him, and healed *them* all.[10]

---

1. Matt. 12 : 17-21.
2. Luke 6 : 12, 13.
3. Mark 3 : 13.
4. Luke 6 : 13.
5. Mark 3 : 14.
6. Matt. 10 : 1.
7. Mark 3 : 15-18.
8. Luke 6 : 15, 16.
9. Mark 3 : 19.
10. Luke 6 : 17-19.

§32—THE SERMON ON THE MOUNT.*

MATTHEW'S VERSION—CHAPTERS 5, 6, 7.

And seeing the multitudes, he went up into the mountain: and when he had sat down, his disciples came unto him: and he opened his mouth and taught them, saying,

Blessed are the poor in spirit: for theirs is the kingdom of heaven.

Blessed are they that mourn: for they shall be comforted.

Blessed are the meek: for they shall inherit the earth.

Blessed are they that hunger and thirst after righteousness: for they shall be filled.

Blessed are the merciful: for they shall obtain mercy.

Blessed are the pure in heart: for they shall see God.

Blessed are the peacemakers: for they shall be called sons of God.

Blessed are they that have been persecuted for righteousness' sake: for theirs is the kingdom of heaven. Blessed are ye when men shall reproach you, and persecute you, and say all manner of evil against you falsely, for my sake. Rejoice, and be exceeding glad: for great is your reward in heaven: for so persecuted they the prophets which were before you.

Ye are the salt of the earth: but if the salt have lost its savour, wherewith shall it be salted? it is thenceforth good for nothing, but to be cast out and trodden under foot of men. Ye are the light of the world. A city set on a hill cannot be hid. Neither do men light a lamp, and put it under the bushel, but on the stand; and it shineth unto all'

---

* *The Sermon on the Mount.*—This is probably the same discourse, at least in the main, as that recorded in the sixth chapter, and in part of the seventh, of St. Luke's Gospel; although doubtless our Lord repeated the substance of his discourse at different times. The apparent discrepancies as to place where the sermon was spoken are not incapable of satisfactory explanation. It would be easy to interweave the account of St. Matthew and St. Luke into a harmonious whole; but this would in large measure mar the familiar beauty of both. It is thought best, therefore, as there is no chronological or doctrinal point involved, to give them separately.

1. Matt. 5: 1-15.

that are in the house. Even so let your light shine before men, that they may see your good works, and glorify your Father which is in heaven.

Think not that I came to destroy the law or the prophets : I came not to destroy, but to fulfil. For verily I say unto you, Till heaven and earth pass away, one jot or one tittle shall in no wise pass away from the law, till all things be accomplished. Whosoever therefore shall break one of these least commandments, and shall teach men so, shall be called least in the kingdom of heaven : but whosoever shall do and teach them, he shall be called great in the kingdom of heaven. For I say unto you, that except your righteousness shall exceed *the righteousness* of the scribes and Pharisees, ye shall in no wise enter into the kingdom of heaven.

Ye have heard that it was said to them of old time, Thou shalt not kill ; and whosoever shall kill shall be in danger of the judgement : but I say unto you, that every one who is angry with his brother shall be in danger of the judgement ; and whosoever shall say to his brother, Raca, shall be in danger of the council ; and whosoever shall say, Thou fool, shall be in danger of the hell of fire. If therefore thou art offering thy gift at the altar, and there rememberest that thy brother hath aught against thee,[1] leave there thy gift before the altar, and go thy way, first be reconciled to thy brother, and then come and offer thy gift. Agree with thine adversary quickly, whiles thou art with him in the way ; lest haply the adversary deliver thee to the judge, and the judge deliver thee to the officer, and thou be cast into prison. Verily I say unto thee, Thou shalt by no means come out thence, till thou have paid the last farthing.

Ye have heard that it was said, Thou shalt not commit adultery : but I say unto you, that every one that lookteh on a woman to lust after her hath committed adultery with her already in his heart. And if thy right eye causeth thee to stumble, pluck it out, and cast it from thee : for it is profitable for thee that one of thy members should perish, and not thy whole body be cast into hell. And if thy right[1]

---

1. Matt. 5 : 16-30.

hand causeth thee to stumble, cut it off, and cast it from thee : for it is profitable for thee that one of thy members should perish, and not thy whole body go into hell. It was said also, Whosoever shall put away his wife, let him give her a writing of divorcement : but I say unto you, that every one that putteth away his wife, saving for the cause of fornication, maketh her an adulteress : and whosoever shall marry her when she is put away committeth adultery.

Again, ye have heard that it was said to them of old time, Thou shalt not forswear thyself, but shalt perform unto the Lord thine oaths : but I say unto you, Swear not at all ; neither by the heaven, for it is the throne of God ; nor by the earth, for it is the footstool of his feet ; nor by Jerusalem, for it is the city of the great King. Neither shalt thou swear by thy head, for thou canst not make one hair white or black. But let your speech be, Yea, yea ; Nay, nay : and whatsoever is more than these is of the evil one.

Ye have heard that it was said, An eye for an eye, and a tooth for a tooth : but I say unto you, Resist not him that is evil : but whosoever smiteth thee on thy right cheek, turn to him the other also. And if any man would go to law with thee, and take away thy coat, let him have thy cloke also. And whosoever shall compel thee to go one mile, go with him twain. Give to him that asketh thee, and from him that would borrow of thee turn not thou away.

Ye have heard that it was said, Thou shalt love thy neighbour, and hate thine enemy : but I say unto you, Love your enemies, pray for them that persecute you, that ye may be sons of your Father which is in heaven : for he maketh his sun to rise on the evil and the good, and sendeth rain on the just and the unjust. For if ye love them that love you, what reward have ye ? do not even the publicans the same ?[1] And if ye salute your brethren only, what do ye more *than others?* do not even the Gentiles the same ?[1]

---

1. Matt. 5 : 31-47.

Ye therefore shall be perfect, as your heavenly Father is perfect.

Take heed that ye do not your righteousness before men, to be seen of them : else ye have no reward with your Father which is in heaven.

When therefore thou doest alms, sound not a trumpet before thee, as the hypocrites do in the synagogues and in the streets, that they may have glory of men.   Verily I say unto you, They have received their reward.   But when thou doest alms, let not thy left hand know what thy right hand doeth : that thine alms may be in secret; and thy Father which seeth in secret shall recompense thee.

And when ye pray, ye shall not be as the hypocrites : for they love to stand and pray in the synagogues and in the corners of the streets, that they may be seen of men. Verily I say unto you, They have received their reward. But thou, when thou prayest, enter into thine inner chamber, and having shut thy door, pray to thy Father which is in secret, and thy Father which seeth in secret shall recompense thee.   And in praying use not vain repetitions, as the Gentiles do : for they think that they shall be heard for their much speaking.   Be not therefore like unto them : for your Father knoweth what things ye have need of, before ye ask him.   After this manner therefore pray ye : Our Father which art in heaven, Hallowed be thy name. Thy kingdom come.   Thy will be done, as in heaven, so on earth.   Give us this day our daily bread.   And forgive us our debts, as we also have forgiven our debtors.   And bring us not into temptation, but deliver us from the evil one.   For if ye forgive men their trespasses, your heavenly Father will also forgive you.   But if ye forgive not men their trespasses, neither will your Father forgive your trespasses.

Moreover when ye fast, be not, as the hypocrites, of a sad countenance : for they disfigure their faces, that they may be seen of men to fast.   Verily I say unto you, They have received their reward.   But thou, when thou fastest,[1]

---

1. Matt. 5 : 48 to Matt. 6 : 1-17.

anoint thy head, and wash thy face; that thou be not seen
of men to fast, but of thy Father which is in secret : and
thy Father, which seeth in secret, shall recompense thee.

Lay not up for yourselves treasures upon the earth, where
moth and rust doth consume, and where thieves break
through and steal : but lay up for yourselves treasures in
heaven, where neither moth nor rust doth consume, and
where thieves do not break through nor steal : for where thy
treasure is, there will thy heart be also.   The lamp of the
body is the eye : if therefore thine eye be single, thy whole
body shall be full of light.   But if thine eye be evil, thy
whole body shall be full of darkness.   If therefore the light
that is in thee be darkness, how great is the darkness !   No
man can serve two masters : for either he will hate the one,
and love the other ; or else he will hold to one, and despise
the other.   Ye cannot serve God and mammon.   Therefore
I say unto you, Be not anxious for your life, what ye shall
eat, or what ye shall drink ; nor yet for your body, what ye
shall put on.   Is not the life more than the food, and the body
than the raiment ?   Behold the birds of the heaven, that
they sow not, neither do they reap, nor gather into barns ;
and your heavenly Father feedeth them.   Are ye not of
much more value than they ?   And which of you by being
anxious can add one cubit unto his stature ?   And why are
ye anxious concerning raiment ?   Consider the lilies of the
field, how they grow ; they toil not, neither do they spin :
yet I say unto you, that even Solomon in all his glory was not
arrayed like one of these.   But if God doth so clothe the grass
of the field, which to-day is, and to-morrow is cast into the
oven, *shall he* not much more *clothe* you, O ye of little faith ?
Be not therefore anxious, saying, What shall we eat ? or,
What shall we drink ? or, Wherewithal shall we be clothed?
For after all these things do the Gentiles seek ; for your
heavenly Father knoweth that ye have need of these things.
But seek ye first his kingdom, and his righteousness ; and
all these things shall be added unto you.   Be not therefore[1]

---

1. Matt. 6 : 18-34.

anxious for the morrow : for the morrow will be anxious for itself. Sufficient unto the day is the evil thereof.

Judge not, that ye be not judged. For with what judgement ye judge, ye shall be judged : and with what measure ye mete, it shall be measured unto you. And why beholdest thou the mote that is in thy brother's eye, but considerest not the beam that is in thine own eye ? Or how wilt thou say to thy brother, Let me cast out the mote out of thine eye ; and lo, the beam is in thine own eye ? Thou hypocrite, cast out first the beam out of thine own eye ; and then shalt thou see clearly to cast out the mote out of thy brother's eye.

Give not that which is holy unto the dogs, neither cast your pearls before the swine, lest haply they trample' them under their feet, and turn and rend you.

Ask, and it shall be given you ; seek, and ye shall find ; knock, and it shall be opened unto you : for every one that asketh receiveth ; and he that seeketh findeth ; and to him that knocketh it shall be opened. Or what man is there of you, who, if his son shall ask him for a loaf will give him a stone ; or if he shall ask for a fish, will give him a serpent ? If ye then, being evil, know how to give good gifts unto your children, how much more shall your Father which is in heaven give good things to them that ask him ? All things therefore whatsoever ye would that men should do unto you, even so do ye also unto them : for this is the law and the prophets.

Enter ye in by the narrow gate : for wide is the gate, and broad is the way, that leadeth to destruction, and many be they that enter in thereby. For narrow is the gate, and straitened the' way, that leadeth unto life, and few be they that find it.

Beware of false prophets, which come to you in sheep's clothing, but inwardly are ravening wolves. By their fruits ye shall know them. Do *men* gather grapes of thorns, or figs of thistles ? Even so every good tree bringeth forth good fruit; but the corrupt tree bringeth forth evil fruit. A good tree cannot bring forth evil -fruit, neither can a[1]

---

1. Matt. 6 : 34 to 7 : 1-18.

corrupt tree bring forth good fruit. Every tree that bringeth not forth good fruit is hewn down, and cast into the fire. Therefore by their fruits ye shall know them. Not every one that saith unto me, Lord, Lord, shall enter into the kingdom of heaven ; but he that doeth the will of my Father which is in heaven. Many will say to me in that day, Lord, Lord, did we not prophesy by thy name, and by thy name cast out devils, and by thy name do many mighty works ? And then will I profess unto them, I never knew you : depart from me, ye that work iniquity. Every one therefore which heareth these words of mine, and doeth them, shall be likened unto a wise man, which built his house upon the rock : and the rain descended, and the floods came, and the winds blew, and beat upon that house ; and it fell not : for it was founded upon the rock. And every one that heareth these words of mine, and doeth them not, shall be likened unto a foolish man, which built his house upon the sand : and the rain descended, and the floods came, and the winds blew, and smote upon that house ; and it fell : and great was the fall thereof.

And it came to pass, when Jesus ended these words, the multitudes were astonished at his teaching : for he taught them as *one* having authority, and not as their scribes.[1]

§33—THE SERMON ON THE MOUNT.

Luke's Version—Luke 6 : 20-36 ; 12 : 22-34 ; 6 : 37-49.

And he lifted up his eyes on his disciples, and said, Blessed *are* ye poor : for yours is the kingdom of God. Blessed *are* ye that hunger now : for ye shall be filled. Blessed *are* ye that weep now : for ye shall laugh. Blessed are ye, when men shall hate you, and when they shall separate you *from their company*, and reproach you, and cast out your name as evil, for the Son of man's sake. Rejoice in that day, and leap *for joy* : for behold, your reward is great in heaven : for in the same manner did their fathers unto the prophets. But woe unto you that are rich ! for ye have received your[2]

---

1. Matt. 7 : 19-29.   2. Luke 6 : 20-24.

consolation. Woe unto you, ye that are full now! for ye shall hunger. Woe *unto you*, ye that laugh now! for ye shall mourn and weep. Woe *unto you*, when all men shall speak well of you! for in the same manner did their fathers to the false prophets.

But I say unto you which hear, Love your enemies, do good to them that hate you, bless them that curse you, pray for them that despitefully use you. To him that smiteth thee on the *one* cheek offer also the other; and from him that taketh away thy cloke withhold not thy coat also. Give to every one that asketh thee; and of him that taketh away thy goods ask them not again. And as ye would that men should do to you, do ye also to them likewise. And if ye love them that love you, what thank have ye? for even sinners love those that love them. And if ye do good to them that do good to you, what thank have ye? for even sinners do the same. And if ye lend to them of whom ye hope to receive, what thank have ye? even sinners lend to sinners, to receive again as much. But love your enemies, and do *them* good, and lend, never despairing; and your reward shall be great, and ye shall be sons of the Most High: for he is kind toward the unthankful and evil. Be ye merciful, even as your Father is merciful.[1]

And he said unto his disciples, Therefore I say unto you, Be not anxious for *your* life, what ye shall eat; nor yet for your body, what ye shall put on. For the life is more than the food, and the body than the raiment. Consider the ravens, that they sow not, neither reap; which have no store-chamber nor barn; and God feedeth them: of how much more value are ye than the birds! And which of you by being anxious can add a cubit unto his stature? If then ye are not able to do even that which is least, why are ye anxious concerning the rest? Consider the lilies, how they grow: they toil not, neither do they spin; yet I say unto you, Even Solomon in all his glory was not arrayed like one of these. But if God doth so clothe the grass in the field, which to-day is, and to-morrow is cast into the oven; how[2]

---

1. Luke 6 : 25-36.   2. Luke 12 : 22-28.

much more *shall he clothe* you, O ye of little faith ? And
seek not ye what ye shall eat, and what ye shall drink,
neither be ye of doubtful mind. For all these things do the
nations of the world seek after : but your Father knoweth
that ye have need of these things. Howbeit seek ye his
kingdom, and these things shall be added unto you. Fear
not, little flock ; for it is your Father's good pleasure to give
you the kingdom. Sell that ye have, and give alms ; make
for yourselves purses which wax not old, a treasure in the
heavens that faileth not, where no thief draweth near, neither
moth destroyeth. For where your treasure is, there will
your heart be also.[1]

And judge not, and ye shall not be judged : and condemn
not, and ye shall not be condemned : release, and ye shall
be released : give, and it shall be given unto you ; good
measure, pressed down, shaken together, running over, shall
they give into your bosom. For with what measure ye mete
it shall be measured to you again.

And he spake also a parable unto them, Can the blind
guide the blind ? shall they not both fall into a pit ? The
disciple is not above his master : but every one when he is
perfected shall be as his master. And why beholdest thou
the mote that is in thy brother's eye, but considerest not the
beam that is in thine own eye ? Or how canst thou say to thy
brother, Brother, let me cast out the mote that is in thine
eye, when thou thyself beholdest not the beam that is in
thine own eye ? Thou hypocrite, cast out first the beam out
of thine own eye, and then shalt thou see clearly to cast out
the mote that is in thy brother's eye. For there is no good tree
that bringeth forth corrupt fruit ; nor again a corrupt tree
that bringeth forth good fruit. For each tree is known by
its own fruit. For of thorns men do not gather figs, nor of
a bramble bush gather they grapes. The good man out of
the good treasure of his heart bringeth forth that which is
good ; and the evil *man* out of the evil *treasure* bringeth
forth that which is evil : for out of the abundance of the
heart his mouth speaketh.[2]

---

1. Luke 12 : 29-34.   2. Luke 6 : 37-45.

And why call ye me, Lord, Lord, and do not the things which I say ? Every one that cometh unto me, and heareth my words, and doeth them, I will shew you to whom he is like : he is like a man building a house, who digged and went deep, and laid a foundation upon the rock : and when a flood arose, the stream brake against that house, and could not shake it : because it had been well builded. But he that heareth, and doeth not, is like a man that built a house upon the earth without a foundation ; against which the stream brake, and straightway it fell in ; and the ruin of that house was great.[1]

§ 34—JESUS HEALS THE CENTURION'S SERVANT AND RAISES A WIDOW'S SON TO LIFE.

After he had ended all his sayings in the ears of the people,[2] when he was come down from the mountain, great multitudes followed him.[3]

[And when he was entered into Capernaum, there came unto him a centurion, beseeching him, and saying, Lord, my servant lieth in the house sick of the palsy, grievously tormented. And he saith unto him, I will come and heal him.][4]

And a certain centurion's servant, who was dear unto him, was sick and at the point of death. And when he heard concerning Jesus, he sent unto him elders of the Jews, asking him that he would come and save his servant. And they, when they came to Jesus, besought him earnestly, saying, He is worthy that thou shouldest do this for him : for he loveth our nation, and himself built us our synagogue. And Jesus went with them. And when he was now not far from the house, the centurion sent friends to him, saying unto him, Lord, trouble not thyself : for I am not worthy that thou shouldest come under my roof : wherefore neither thought I myself worthy to come unto thee : but say the word, and my servant shall be healed. For I also am a man

---

1. Luke 6 : 46-49. 3. Matt. 8 : 1. 4. Matt. 8 : 5-7.
2. Luke 7 : 1.

set under authority, having under myself soldiers: and I say
to this one, Go, and he goeth; and to another, Come, and
he cometh; and to my servant, Do this, and he doeth it.
And when Jesus heard these things, he marvelled at him,
and turned and said unto the multitude that followed him,
I say unto you, I have not found so great faith, no, not in
Israel.[1] And I say unto you, that many shall come from the
east and the west, and shall sit down with Abraham, and
Isaac, and Jacob, in the kingdom of heaven: but the sons of
the kingdom shall be cast forth into the outer darkness:
there shall be the weeping and gnashing of teeth. And
Jesus said unto the centurion, Go thy way; as thou hast
believed, so be it done unto thee. And the servant was
healed in that hour.[2] [And they that were sent, returning
to the house, found the servant whole.[3]]

And it came to pass soon afterwards, that he went to a
city called Nain; and his disciples went with him, and a
great multitude. Now when he drew near to the gate of the
city, behold, there was carried out one that was dead, the
only son of his mother, and she was a widow: and much
people of the city was with her. And when the Lord saw
her, he had compassion on her, and said unto her, Weep
not. And he came nigh and touched the bier: and the
bearers stood still. And he said, Young man, I say unto
thee, Arise. And he that was dead sat up, and began to
speak. And he gave him to his mother. And fear took
hold on all: and they glorified God, saying, A great prophet
is arisen among us: and God hath visited his people. And
this report went forth concerning him in the whole of Judæa,
and all the region round about.[4]

---

1. Luke 7 : 2-9. 3. Luke 7 : 10. 4. Luke 7 : 11-17.
2. Matt. 8 : 11-13.

§35—THE TESTIMONY OF JESUS CONCERNING
JOHN THE BAPTIST.

And the disciples of John told him of all these things[1] in the prison.[2]   And John calling unto him two of his disciples sent them to the Lord, saying, Art thou he that cometh, or look we for another ?   And when the men were come unto him, they said, John the Baptist hath sent us unto thee, saying, Art thou he that cometh, or look we for another ? In that hour he cured many of diseases and plagues and evil spirits ; and on many that were blind he bestowed sight. And he answered and said unto them, Go your way, and tell John what things ye have seen and heard ; the blind receive their sight, the lame walk, the lepers are cleansed, and the deaf hear, the dead are raised up, the poor have good tidings preached to them.   And blessed is he, whosoever shall find none occasion of stumbling in me.

And when the messengers of John were departed, he be-gan to say unto the multitudes concerning John, What went ye out into the wilderness to behold ? a reed shaken with the wind ?   But what went ye out to see ? a man clothed in soft raiment ?   Behold, they which are gorgeously apparelled, and live delicately, are in kings' courts.   But what went ye out to see ? a prophet ?   Yea, I say unto you, and much more than a prophet.   This is he of whom it is written,

Behold, I send my messenger before thy face,
Who shall prepare thy way before thee.[3]

Verily I say unto you, Among them that are born of women there hath not arisen a greater than John the Baptist : yet he that is but little in the kingdom of heaven is greater than he. And from the days of John the Baptist until now the kingdom of heaven suffereth violence, and men of violence take it by force.   For all the prophets and the law prophesied until John.   And if ye are willing to receive *it*, this is Elijah, which is to come.   He that hath ears to hear, let him hear.[4]

---

1. Luke 7 : 18.   3. Luke 7 : 19-27   4. Matt. 11 : 11-15.
2. Matt. 11 : 2.

4

I say unto you, Among them that are born of women there is none greater than John : yet he that is but little in the kingdom of God is greater than he. And all the people when they heard, and the publicans, justified God, being baptized with the baptism of John. But the Pharisees and the lawyers rejected for themselves the counsel of God, being not baptized of him. Whereunto then shall I liken the men of this generation, and to what are they like ? They are like unto children that sit in the marketplace, and call one to another; which say, We piped unto you, and ye did not dance ; we wailed, and ye did not weep. For John the Baptist is come eating no bread nor drinking wine ; and ye say, He hath a devil. The Son of man is come eating and drinking; and ye say, Behold, a gluttonous man, and a wine-bibber, a friend of publicans and sinners ! And wisdom is justified of all her children.[1]

§36—A WOMAN ANOINTS THE FEET OF JESUS IN THE HOUSE OF SIMON THE PHARISEE.

And one of the Pharisees desired him that he would eat with him. And he entered into the Pharisee's house, and sat down to meat. And behold, a woman which was in the city, a sinner ; and when she knew that he was sitting at meat in the Pharisee's house, she brought an alabaster cruse of ointment, and standing behind at his feet, weeping, she began to wet his feet with her tears, and wiped them with the hair of her head, and kissed his feet, and anointed them with the ointment. Now when the Pharisee which had bidden him saw it, he spake within himself, saying, This man, if he were a prophet, would have perceived who and what manner of woman this is which toucheth him, that she is a sinner. And Jesus answering said unto him, Simon, I have somewhat to say unto thee. And he saith, Master, say on. A certain lender had two debtors : the one owed five hundred pence, and the other fifty. When they had not *wherewith* to pay, he forgave them both. Which of them

---

1. Luke 7 : 28-35.

therefore will love him most ? Simon answered and said, He, I suppose, to whom he forgave the most. And he said unto him, Thou hast rightly judged. And turning to the woman, he said unto Simon, Seest thou this woman ? I entered into thine house, thou gavest me no water for my feet : but she hath wetted my feet with her tears, and wiped them with her hair. Thou gavest me no kiss : but she, since the time I came in, hath not ceased to kiss my feet. My head with oil thou didst not anoint : but she hath anointed my feet with ointment. Wherefore I say unto thee, Her sins, which are many, are forgiven ; for she loved much : but to whom little is forgiven, *the same* loveth little. And he said unto her, Thy sins are forgiven. And they that sat at meat with him began to say within themselves, Who is this that even forgiveth sins ? And he said unto the woman, Thy faith hath saved thee ; go in peace.[1]

§ 37—JESUS HEALS A DEMONIAC AND REBUKES THE PHARISEES.

And it came to pass soon afterwards, that he went about through cities and villages, preaching and bringing the good tidings of the kingdom of God, and with him the twelve, and certain women which had been healed of evil spirits and infirmities, Mary that was called Magdalene, from whom seven devils had gone out, and Joanna the wife of Chuza, Herod's steward, and Susanna, and many others, which ministered unto them of their substance.[2]

And he cometh into a house. And the multitude cometh together again, so that they could not so much as eat bread. And when his friends heard it, they went out to lay hold on him : for they said, He is beside himself.[3]

Then was brought unto him one possessed with a devil, blind and dumb : and he healed him, insomuch that[4] when the devil was gone out[5] the dumb man spake and saw. And all the multitudes were amazed, and said, Is this the son of

---

1. Luke 7 : 36-50.   3. Mark 3 : 20, 21.   5. Luke 11 : 14.
2. Luke 8 : 1-3.   4. Matt. 12 : 22.

David ? But when[1] the scribes which were come down from
Jerusalem[2] and the Pharisees heard it, they said, This man doth
not cast out devils, but by Beelzebub the prince of the devils.
And knowing their thoughts he[3] called them unto him, and
said unto them in parables, How can Satan cast out Satan ?[4]
Every kingdom divided against itself is brought to desolation ; and every city or house divided against itself shall not
stand : and if Satan casteth out Satan, he is divided against
himself ; how then shall his kingdom stand ? And if I by
Beelzebub cast out devils, by whom do your sons cast them
out ? therefore shall they be your judges. But if I by the
Spirit of God cast out devils, then is the kingdom of God
come upon you.[5] When the strong *man* fully armed guardeth
his own court, his goods are in peace : but when a stronger
than he shall come upon him, and overcome him, he taketh
from him his whole armour wherein he trusted, and divideth
his spoils. He that is not with me is against me ; and he
that gathereth not with me scattereth.[6] Therefore I say
unto you, Every sin and blasphemy shall be forgiven unto
men,[7] and their blasphemies wherewith soever they shall
blaspheme,[8] but the blasphemy against the Spirit shall not
be forgiven, And whosoever shall speak a word against the
Son of man, it shall be forgiven him ; but whosoever shall
speak against the Holy Spirit, it shall not be forgiven him,
neither in this world, nor in that which is to come ;[9] but is
guilty of an eternal sin : because they said, He hath an
unclean spirit.[10]

Either make the tree good, and its fruit good ; or make
the tree corrupt, and its fruit corrupt : for the tree is known
by its fruit. Ye offspring of vipers, how can ye, being evil,
speak good things ? for out of the abundance of the heart the
mouth speaketh. The good man out of his good treasure
bringeth forth good things : and the evil man out of his evil
treasure bringeth forth evil things. And I say unto you,
that every idle word that men shall speak, they shall give

---

1. Matt. 12 : 22, 23.   5. Matt. 12 : 25-28.   8. Mark 3 : 28.
2. Mark 3 : 22.   6. Luke 11 : 21-23.   9. Matt. 12 : 31, 32.
3. Matt. 12 : 24, 25.   7. Matt. 12 : 31.   10. Mark 3 : 30.
4. Mark 3 : 23.

account thereof in the day of judgement. For by thy words thou shalt be justified, and by thy words thou shalt be condemned.

Then certain of the scribes and Pharisees answered him, saying, Master, we would see a sign from thee.[1]

And when the multitudes were gathered together unto him, he began to say, This generation is an evil[2] and adulterous[3] generation : it seeketh after a sign ; and there shall no sign be given to it but the sign of Jonah[4] the prophet[5]. For even as Jonah became a sign unto the Ninevites, so shall also the Son of man be to this generation.[6] For as Jonah was three days and three nights in the belly of the whale ; so shall the Son of man be three days and three nights in the heart of the earth. The men of Nineveh shall stand up in the judgement with this generation, and shall condemn it : for they repented at the preaching of Jonah ; and behold, a greater than Jonah is here. The queen of the south shall rise up in the judgement with this generation, and shall condemn it : for she came from the ends of the earth to hear the wisdom of Solomon ; and behold, a greater than Solomon is here. But the unclean spirit, when he is gone out of the man, passeth through waterless places, seeking rest, and findeth it not. Then he saith, I will return into my house whence I came out ; and when he is come, he findeth it empty, swept, and garnished. Then goeth he, and taketh with himself seven other spirits more evil than himself, and they enter in and dwell there : and the last state of that man becometh worse than the first. Even so shall it be also unto this evil generation.[7]

While he was yet speaking to the multitudes, behold, his mother and his brethren stood without, seeking to speak to him :[8] and they could not come at him for the crowd.[9] And a multitude was sitting about him ; and they say unto him, Behold, thy mother and thy brethren[10] stand without, seeking

---

1. Matt. 12 : 33-38.
2. Luke 11 : 29.
3. Matt. 12 : 39.
4. Luke 11 : 29.
5. Matt. 12 : 39.
6. Luke 2 : 30.
7. Matt. 12 : 40-45.
8. Matt. 12 : 46.
9. Luke 8 : 19.
10. Mark 3 : 3'.

to speak to thee.   But he answered and said unto him that told him, Who is my mother? and Who are my brethren?[1] And looking round on them who sat about him,[2] he stretched forth his hand toward his disciples, and said, Behold, my mother and my brethren! For whosoever shall do the will of my Father which is in heaven, he is my brother, and sister, and mother.[3]

§ 38——PARABLES OF THE SOWER, THE LAMP, THE SEED.

On that day went Jesus out of the house, and sat by the sea side,[4] and began to teach by the sea side,[5] and there were gathered unto him great multitudes,[6] and they of every city resorted unto him,[7] so that he entered into a boat, and sat in the sea ; and all the multitude were by the sea on the land.   And he taught them many things in parables, and said unto them in his teaching, Hearken : Behold, the sower went forth to sow : and it came to pass, as he sowed, some *seed* fell by the way side[8] and it was trodden under foot,[9] and the birds came and devoured it.   And other fell on the rocky *ground*, where it had not much earth ; and straight-way it sprang up, because it had no deepness of earth : and when the sun was risen, it was scorched ; and because it had no root, it withered away.   And other fell among the thorns, and the thorns grew up, and choked it, and it yielded no fruit.   And others fell into the good ground, and yielded fruit, growing up and increasing ; and brought forth, thirtyfold, and sixtyfold, and a hundredfold.   And he said, Who hath ears to hear, let him hear.

And when he was alone, they that were about him with the twelve asked of him,[10] Why speakest thou unto them in parables ?   And he answered and said unto them, Unto you it is given to know the mysteries of the kingdom of heaven,

---

1. Matt. 12 : 47, 48.
2. Mark 3 : 34.
3. Matt. 12 : 49, 50.
4. Matt. 13 : 1.

5. Mark 4 : 1.
6. Matt. 13 : 2.
7. Luke 8 : 4.

8. Mark 4 : 1-4.
9. Luke 8 : 5.
10. Mark 4 : 4-10.

but to them it is not given.[1] Unto them that are without, all things are done in parables.[2] For whosoever hath, to him shall be given, and he shall have abundance : but whosoever hath not, from him shall be taken away even that which he hath. Therefore speak I to them in parables ; because seeing they see not, and hearing they hear not, neither do they understand,[3] lest haply they should turn again, and it should be forgiven them.[4] And unto them is fulfilled the prophecy of Isaiah, which saith,

By hearing ye shall hear, and shall in no wise under-
> stand ;
And seeing ye shall see, and shall in no wise perceive :
For this people's heart is waxed gross,
And their ears are dull of hearing,
And their eyes they have closed ;
Lest haply they should perceive with their eyes,
And hear with their ears,
And understand with their heart,
And should turn again,
And I should heal them.

But blessed are your eyes, for they see ; and your ears, for they hear. For verily I say unto you, that many prophets and righteous men desired to see the things which ye see, and saw them not ; and to hear the things which ye hear, and heard them not.[5]

And he saith unto them, Know ye not this parable ? and how shall ye know all the parables ?[6] The seed is the word of God.[7] The sower soweth the word. And these are they by the way side, where the word is sown ; and when they have heard, straightway cometh Satan, and taketh away the word[8] from their heart,[9] which hath been sown in them,[10] that they may not believe and be saved.[11] And these in like manner are they that are sown upon the rocky *places*, who, when they have heard the word, straightway receive it with joy ; and they have no root in themselves, but endure for a

1. Matt. 13: 10, 11.
2. Mark 4 : 11.
3. Matt. 13 : 12, 13.
4. Mark 4 : 12.
5. Matt. 13 : 14-17.
6. Mark 4 : 13.
7. Luke 8 : 11.
8. Mark 4 : 14, 15.
9. Luke 8 : 12.
10. Mark 4 : 15.
11. Luke 8 : 12.

while ; then, when tribulation or persecution ariseth because of the word, straightway they stumble.[1] [Which for a while believe, and in time of temptation fall away.[2]] And others are they that are sown among the thorns ; these are they that have heard the word, and the cares of the world, and the deceitfulness of riches, and the lusts of other things entering in, choke the word, and it becometh unfruitful ;[3] [and as they go on their way they are choked with cares and riches and pleasures of *this* life, and bring no fruit to perfection].[4] And those are they that were sown upon the good ground ; such[5] as in an honest and good heart, having heard the word, hold it fast, and bring forth fruit with patience,[6] thirtyfold, and sixtyfold, and a hundredfold.

And he said unto them,[7] No man, when he hath lighted a lamp, covereth it with a vessel, or putteth it under a bed ; but putteth it on a stand, that they which enter in may see the light. For nothing is hid, that shall not be made manifest ; nor *anything* secret, that shall not be known and come to light.[8] If any man hath ears to hear, let him hear. And he said unto them, Take heed what ye hear : with what measure ye mete it shall be measured unto you : and more shall be given unto you. For he that hath, to him shall be given : and he that hath not, from him shall be taken away even that which[9] he thinketh he hath.[10]

And he said, So is the kingdom of God, as if a man should cast seed upon the earth ; and should sleep and rise night and day, and the seed should spring up and grow, he knoweth not how. The earth beareth fruit of herself ; first the blade, then the ear, then the full corn in the ear. But when the fruit is ripe, straightway he putteth forth the sickle, because the harvest is come.[11]

---

1. Mark 4 : 16, 17.	5. Mark 4 : 20.	9. Mark 4 : 23-25.
2. Luke 8 : 13.	6. Luke 8 : 15.	10. Luke 8 : 18.
3. Mark 4 : 18, 19.	7. Mark 4 : 20, 21.	11. Mark 4 : 26-29.
4. Luke 4 : 14.	8. Luke 8 : 16, 17.	

§ 39—JESUS DISCOURSES ON TRÚE BLESSEDNESS, ON FORMALISM, AND ON GODLINESS.

And it came to pass, as he said these things, a certain woman out of the multitude lifted up her voice, and said unto him, Blessed is the womb that bare thee, and the breasts which thou didst suck. But he said, Yea rather, blessed are they that hear the word of God, and keep it.[1]

No man, when he hath lighted a lamp, putteth it in a cellar, neither under the bushel, but on the stand, that they which enter in may see the light. The lamp of thy body is thine eye : when thine eye is single, thy whole body also is full of light ; but when it is evil, thy body also is full of darkness. Look therefore whether the light that is in thee be not darkness. If therefore thy whole body be full of light, having no part dark, it shall be wholly full of light, as when the lamp with its bright shining doth give thee light.

Now as he spake, a Pharisee asketh him to dine with him : and he went in, and sat down to meat. And when the Pharisee saw it, he marvelled that he had not first washed before dinner. And the Lord said unto him, Now do ye Pharisees cleanse the outside of the cup and of the platter ; but your inward part is full of extortion and wickedness. Ye foolish ones, did not he that made the outside make the inside also ? Howbeit give for alms those things which are within ; and behold, all things are clean unto you.

But woe unto you Pharisees ! for ye tithe mint and rue and every herb, and pass over judgement and the love of God : but these ought ye to have done, and not to leave the other undone. Woe unto you Pharisees ! for ye love the chief seats in the synagogues, and the salutations in the marketplaces. Woe unto you ! for ye are as the tombs which appear not, and the men that walk over *them* know it not.

And one of the lawyers answering saith unto him, Master, in saying this thou reproachest us also. And he said, Woe[2]

---

1. Luke 11 : 27, 28.   2. Luke 11 : 33-46.

unto you lawyers also ! for ye lade men with burdens grievous to be borne, and ye yourselves touch not the burdens
with one of your fingers.   Woe unto you ! for ye build the
tombs of the prophets, and your fathers killed them.   So ye
are witnesses and consent unto the works of your fathers :
for they killed them, and ye build *their tombs.*   Therefore
also said the wisdom of God, I will send unto them prophets
and apostles ; and *some* of them they shall kill and persecute ; that the blood of all the prophets, which was shed
from the foundation of the world, may be required of this
generation; from the blood of Abel unto the blood of
Zachariah, who perished between the altar and the sanctuary:
yea, I say unto you, it shall be required of this generation.
Woe unto you lawyers ! for ye took away the key of knowledge : ye entered not in yourselves, and them that were
entering in ye hindered.

And when he was come out from thence, the scribes and
the Pharisees began to press upon *him* vehemently, and to
provoke him to speak of many things ; laying wait for him,
to catch something out of his mouth.[1]

In the mean time, when the many thousands of the multitude were gathered together, insomuch that they trode one
upon another, he began to say unto his disciples first of all,
Beware ye of the leaven of the Pharisees, which is hypocrisy.
But there is nothing covered up, that shall not be revealed :
and hid, that shall not be known.   Wherefore whatsoever
ye have said in the darkness shall be heard in the light; and
what ye have spoken in the ear in the inner chambers shall
be proclaimed upon the housetops.   And I say unto you my
friends, Be not afraid of them which kill the body, and after
that have no more that they can do.   But I will warn you
whom ye shall fear : Fear him, which after he hath killed
hath power to cast into hell ; yea, I say unto you, Fear him.
Are not five sparrows sold for two farthings ? and not one of
them is forgotten in the sight of God.   But the very hairs of
your head are all numbered.   Fear not : ye are of more
value than many sparrows.   And I say unto you, Every one[2]

---

1 Luke 11 : 46-54.   2. Luke 12 : 1-8.

who shall confess me before men, him shall the Son of man also confess before the angels of God : but he that denieth me in the presence of men shall be denied in the presence of the angels of God. And every one who shall speak a word against the Son of man, it shall be forgiven him : but unto him that blasphemeth against the Holy Spirit it shall not be forgiven. And when they bring you before the synagogues, and the rulers, and the authorities, be not anxious how or what ye shall answer, or what ye shall say : for the Holy Spirit shall teach you in that very hour what ye ought to say.[1]

§ 40—THE PARABLES OF THE SELF-DELUDED RICH MAN, AND OF THE SERVANTS AND THE STEWARD WAITING FOR THEIR LORD.

And one of the multitude said unto him, Master, bid my brother divide the inheritance with me. But he said unto him, Man, who made me a judge or a divider over you ? And he said unto them, Take heed, and keep yourselves from all covetousness : for a man's life consisteth not in the abundance of the things which he possesseth. And he spake a parable unto them, saying, The ground of a certain rich man brought forth plentifully : and he reasoned within himself, saying, What shall I do, because I have not where to bestow my fruits ? And he said, This will I do : I will pull down my barns, and build greater ; and there will I bestow all my corn and my goods. And I will say to my soul, Soul, thou hast much goods laid up for many years ; take thine ease, eat, drink, be merry. But God said unto him, Thou foolish one, this night is thy soul required of thee ; and the things which thou hast prepared, whose shall they be ? So is he that layeth up treasure for himself, and is not rich toward God.[2]

Let your loins be girded about, and your lamps burning ; and be ye yourselves like unto men looking for their lord,

---

1. Luke 12 : 9-12.   2. Luke 12 : 13-21.

when he shall return from the marriage feast ; that, when
he cometh and knocketh, they may straightway open unto
him.   Blessed are those servants, whom the lord when he
cometh shall find watching : verily I say unto you, that he
shall gird himself, and make them sit down to meat, and
shall come and serve them.   And if he shall come in the
second watch, and if in the third, and find *them* so, blessed
are those *servants*.   But know this, that if the master of the
house had known in what hour the thief was coming, he
would have watched, and not have left his house to be
broken through.   Be ye also ready : for in an hour that ye
think not the Son of man cometh.

And Peter said, Lord, speakest thou this parable unto us,
or even unto all ? And the Lord said, Who then is the
faithful and wise steward, whom his lord shall set over his
household, to give them their portion of food in due season ?
Blessed is that servant, whom his lord when he cometh
shall find so doing.   Of a truth I say unto you, that he will
set him over all that he hath.   But if that servant shall say
in his heart, My lord delayeth his coming ; and shall begin
to beat the menservants and the maidservants, and to eat
and drink, and to be drunken ; the lord of that servant
shall come in a day when he expecteth not, and in an hour
when he knoweth not, and shall cut him asunder, and
appoint his portion with the unfaithful.   And that servant,
which knew his lord's will, and made not ready, nor did
according to his will, shall be beaten with many *stripes* ; but
he that knew not, and did things worthy of stripes, shall be
beaten with few *stripes*.   And to whomsoever much is given,
of him shall much be required : and to whom they commit
much, of him will they ask the more.[1]

---

1. Luke 12 : 35-48.

§ 41—JESUS FORETELLS THE PERSECUTION OF HIS DISCIPLES.

I came to cast fire upon the earth ; and what will I, if it is already kindled ? But I have a baptism to be baptized with ; and how am I straitened till it be ˙accomplished ! Think ye that I am come to give peace in the earth ? I tell you, Nay ; but rather division : for there shall be from henceforth five in one house divided, three against two, and two against three. They shall be divided, father against son, and son against father ; mother against daughter, and daughter against her mother ; mother in law against her daughter in law, and daughter in law against her mother in law.

And he said to the multitudes also, When ye see a cloud rising in the west, straightway ye say, There cometh a shower ; and so it cometh to pass. And when *ye see* a south wind blowing, ye say, There will be a scorching heat ; and it cometh to pass. Ye hypocrites, ye know how to interpret the face of the earth and the heaven ; but how is it that ye know not how to interpret this time ? And why even of yourselves judge ye not what is right ? For as thou art going with thine adversary before the magistrate, on the way give diligence to be quit of him ; lest haply he hale thee unto the judge, and the judge shall deliver thee to the officer, and the officer shall cast thee into prison. I say unto thee, Thou shalt by no means come out thence, till thou have paid the very last mite.[1]

§ 42—THE SLAUGHTER OF THE GALILÆANS.
PARABLE OF THE FIG TREE.

Now there were some present at that very season which told him of the Galilæans, whose blood Pilate had mingled with their sacrifices. And he answered and said unto them, Think ye that these Galilæans were sinners above all the Galilæans, because they have suffered these things ? I tell

---

1. Luke 12 : 49-59.

you, Nay : but, except ye repent, ye shall all in like manner perish. Or those eighteen, upon whom the tower in Siloam fell, and killed them, think ye that they were offenders above all the men that dwell in Jerusalem ? I tell you, Nay : but, except ye repent, ye shall all likewise perish.

And he spake this parable ; A certain man had a fig tree planted in his vineyard ; and he came seeking fruit thereon, and found none. And he said unto the vinedresser, Behold, these three years I come seeking fruit on this fig tree, and find none : cut it down ; why doth it also cumber the ground ? And he answering saith unto him, Lord, let it alone this year also, till I shall dig about it, and dung it : and if it bear fruit thenceforth, *well* ; but if not, thou shalt cut it down.[1]

§ 43—JESUS HEALS AN INFIRM WOMAN ON THE SABBATH DAY.

And he was teaching in one of the synagogues on the sabbath day. And behold, a woman which had a spirit of infirmity eighteen years ; and she was bowed together, and could in no wise lift herself up. And when Jesus saw her, he called her, and said to her, Woman, thou art loosed from thine infirmity. And he laid his hands upon her : and immediately she was made straight, and glorified God. And the ruler of the synagogue, being moved with indignation because Jesus had healed on the sabbath, answered and said to the multitude, There are six days in which men ought to work : in them therefore come and be healed, and not on the day of the sabbath. But the Lord answered him, and said, Ye hypocrites, doth not each one of you on the sabbath loose his ox or his ass from the stall, and lead him away to watering ? And ought not this woman, being a daughter of Abraham, whom Satan had bound, lo, *these* eighteen years, to have been loosed from this bond on the day of the sabbath ? And as he said these things, all his adversaries were put to shame : and all the multitude rejoiced for all the glorious things that were done by him.[2]

---

1. Luke 13 : 1-9.   2. Luke 13 : 10-17.

§ 44—THE PARABLES OF THE MUSTARD SEED—THE LEAVEN — THE WHEAT AND TARES — THE TREASURE HID IN A FIELD—THE PEARL OF GREAT PRICE—THE NET CAST INTO THE SEA.

And he said, How shall we liken the kingdom of God ? or in what parable shall we set it forth ? It is like a grain of mustard seed, which, when it is sown upon the earth, though it be less than all the seeds that are upon the earth, yet when it is sown, groweth up, and becometh greater than all the herbs, and putteth out great branches ; so that the birds of the heaven can lodge under the shadow thereof.[1] And again he said, Whereunto shall I liken the kingdom of God ? It is like unto leaven, which a woman took and hid in three measures of meal, till it was all leavened.[2]

Another parable set he before them, saying, The kingdom of heaven is likened unto a man that sowed good seed in his field : but while men slept, his enemy came and sowed tares also among the wheat, and went away. But when the blade sprang up, and brought forth fruit, then appeared the tares also. And the servants of the householder came and said unto him, Sir, didst thou not sow good seed in thy field ! whence then hath it tares ? And he said unto them, An enemy hath done this. And the servants say unto him, Wilt thou then that we go and gather them up ? But he saith, Nay ; lest haply while ye gather up the tares, ye root up the wheat with them. Let both grow together until the harvest ? and in the time of the harvest I will say to the reapers, Gather up first the tares, and bind them in bundles to burn them : but gather the wheat into my barn.[3]

All these things spake Jesus in parables unto the multitudes ; and without a parable spake he nothing unto them : that it might be fulfilled which was spoken by the prophet, saying,

---

1. Mark 4 : 30-34.   2. Luke 13 : 20, 21.   3. Matt. 13 : 24-30.

I will open my mouth in parables ;
I will utter things hidden from the foundation of the
   world.[1]

And with many such parables spake he the word unto them,
as they were able to hear it : and without a parable spake he
not unto them : but privately to his own disciples he ex-
pounded all things.[2]

Then he left the multitudes, and went into the house : and
his disciples came unto him, saying, Explain unto us the
parable of the tares of the field. And he answered and said,
He that soweth the good seed is the Son of man ; and the
field is the world ; and the good seed, these are the sons of
the kingdom ; and the tares are the sons of the evil *one* ; and
the enemy that sowed them is the devil : and the harvest is
the end of the world ; and the reapers are angels. As therefore the tares are gathered up and burned with fire ; so shall
it be in the end of the world. The Son of man shall send
forth his angels, and they shall gather out of his kingdom all
things that cause stumbling, and them that do iniquity, and
shall cast them into the furnace of fire : there shall be weeping and gnashing of teeth. Then shall the righteous shine
forth as the sun in the kingdom of their father. He that
hath ears, let him hear.

The kingdom of heaven is like unto a treasure hidden in a
field ; which a man found, and hid ; and in his joy he goeth
and selleth all that he hath, and buyeth that field.

Again, the kingdom of heaven is like unto a man that is
a merchant seeking goodly pearls : and having found one
pearl of great price, he went and sold all that he had, and
bought it.

Again, the kingdom of heaven is like unto a net, that was
cast into the sea, and gathered of every kind : which, when
it was filled, they drew up on the beach ; and they sat down,
and gathered the good into vessels, but the bad they cast
away. So shall it be in the end of the world : the angels
shall come forth, and sever the wicked from among the[3]

---

1. Matt. 13 : 34, 35.   2. Mark 4 : 33, 34.   3. Matt. 13 : 36-49.

righteous, and shall cast them into the furnace of fire : there shall be the weeping and gnashing of teeth.

Have ye understood all these things ? They say unto him, Yea. And he said unto them, Therefore every scribe who hath been made a disciple to the kingdom of heaven is like unto a man that is a householder, which bringeth forth out of his treasure things new and old.

And it came to pass, when Jesus had finished these parables, he departed thence.[1]

§ 45—JESUS STILLS THE STORM ON THE SEA OF GALILEE.

And on that day, when even was come, when Jesus saw great multitudes about him, he gave commandment to depart unto the other side. And there came a scribe, and said unto him, Master, I will follow thee whithersoever thou goest. And Jesus saith unto him, The foxes have holes, and the birds of the heaven *have* nests ; but the Son of man hath not where to lay his head. And another of the disciples said unto him, Lord, suffer me first to go and bury my father. But Jesus saith unto him, Follow me ; and leave the dead to bury their own dead.

And when he was entered into a boat, his disciples followed him.[3] [And leaving the multitude, they take him with them, even as he was, in the boat. And other boats were with him.[4]] And he said unto them, Let us go over unto the other side of the lake : and they launched forth. But as they sailed he fell asleep : and there came down a storm of wind on the lake ; and they were filling *with water*, and were in jeopardy.[5]

[And there ariseth a great storm of wind, and the waves beat into the boat, insomuch that the boat was now filling.] And he himself was in the stern, asleep on the cushion : and they awake him, and say unto him,[6] Save, Lord,[7] Master,

---

1. Matt. 13: 49-53.
2. Mark 4 : 35.
3. Matt. 8: 18-23.
4. Mark 4 : 36.
5. Luke 8 : 22, 23.
6. Mark 4 : 37, 38,
7. Matt. 8 : 25.

5

carest thou not that we perish? And he awoke, and rebuked the wind[1] and the raging of the water,[2] and said unto
the sea, Peace, be still. And the wind ceased, and there
was a great calm. And he said unto them, Why are ye fearful? have ye not yet faith?[3] And being afraid, they marvelled, saying one to another, Who then is this, that he
commandeth even the winds and the water, and they obey
him?[4]

§46—JESUS HEALS TWO DEMONIACS.

And when he was come to the other side into the country
of the Gadarenes,[5] when he was come out of the boat,
straightway there met him out of the tombs a man with an
unclean spirit, who had his dwelling in the tombs : and no
man could any more bind him, no, not with a chain ; because
that he had been often bound with fetters and chains, and
the chains had been rent asunder by him, and the fetters
broken in pieces : and no man had strength to tame him.[6]
And for a long time he had worn no clothes, and abode not
in *any* house, but in the tombs.[7] And always, night and
day, in the tombs and in the mountains, he was crying out,
and cutting himself with stones. And when he saw Jesus
from afar, he ran[8] and fell down before him[9] and worshipped
him, and crying out with a loud voice, he saith, What have
I to do with thee, Jesus, thou Son of the Most High God?
I adjure thee by God, torment me not.[10] For he commanded
the unclean spirit to come out from the man. For often-
times it had seized him : and he was kept under guard, and
bound with chains and fetters ; and breaking the bands
asunder, he was driven of the devil into the deserts. And
Jesus asked him, What is thy name? And he said, Legion ;
for many devils were entered into him. And they entreated
him that he would not command them to depart into the
abyss. Now there was there a herd of many swine feeding
on the mountain.[11] And they besought him, saying, Send us

---

1. Mark 4 : 39.
2. Luke 8 : 24.
3. Mark 4 : 39, 40.
4. Luke 8 : 25.

5. Matt. 8 : 1.
6. Mark 5 : 1-4.
7. Luke 8 : 27.
8. Mark 5 : 5, 6.

9. Luke 8 : 28.
10. Mark 5 : 7.
11. Luke 8 : 29-32.

into the swine, that we may enter into them. And he gave them leave. And the unclean spirits came out, and entered into the swine : and the herd rushed down the steep into the sea, *in number* about two thousand ; and they were choked in the sea.[1] And when they that fed them saw what had come to pass,[2] they went away into the city, and told everything, and what was befallen to them that were possessed with devils. And behold, all the city came out to meet Jesus.[3] And they came to see what it was that had come to pass. And they come to Jesus, and behold him that was possessed with devils sitting, clothed and in his right mind[4] at the feet of Jesus,[5] *even* him that had the legion : and they were afraid. And they that saw it declared unto them how it befell him that was possessed with devils, and concerning the swine.[6] And all the people of the country of the Gerasenes round about asked him to depart from them ; for they were holden with great fear.[7]

And as he was entering into the boat, he that had been possessed with devils besought him that he might be with him. And he suffered him not, but saith unto him, Go to thy house unto thy friends, and tell them how great things the Lord hath done for thee, and *how* he had mercy on thee. And he went his way, and began to publish in Decapolis how great things Jesus had done for him : and all men did marvel.

And when Jesus had crossed over again in the boat unto the other side[8] and came into his own city,[9] a great multitude was gathered into him[10] [and] welcomed him ; for they were all waiting for him ;[11] and he was by the sea.[12]

---

1. Mark 5 : 12, 13.
2. Luke 8 : 34.
3. Matt. 8 : 33, 34.
4. Mark 5 : 14, 15.
5. Luke 8 : 35.
6. Mark 5 : 15, 16.
7. Luke 8 : 37.
8. Mark 5 : 18-21.
9. Matt. 9 : 1.
10. Mark 1 : 21.
11. Luke 8 : 40.
12. Mark 5 : 21.

§ 47—JESUS RAISES TO LIFE THE DEAD DAUGHTER
OF JAIRUS, HEALS A WOMAN HAVING AN
ISSUE OF BLOOD, TWO BLIND MEN AND A
DUMB DEMONIAC.

While he spake these things unto them, behold, there
came[1] one of the rulers of the synagogue, Jairus by name ;
and seeing him,[2] he fell down at Jesus' feet, and besought him to come into his house ; for he had an only
daughter, about twelve years of age, and she lay a dying.[3]
And [he] worshipped him, saying,[4] My little daughter is at
the point of death : *I pray thee*, that thou come and lay thy
hands on her, that she may be made whole, and live.   And
he went with him ; and a great multitude followed him, and
they thronged him.

And a woman, which had an issue of blood twelve years,
and had suffered many things of many physicians, and had
spent all that she had, and was nothing bettered, but rather
grew worse, having heard the things concerning Jesus, came
in the crowd behind, and touched[5] the border of[6] his
garment.   For she said, If I touch but his garments, I shall
be made whole.   And straightway the fountain of her blood
was dried up ; and she felt in her body that she was healed
of her plague.   And straightway Jesus, perceiving in himself that the power *proceeding* from him had gone forth,
turned him about in the crowd, and said, Who touched my
garments ?[7]   And when all denied, Peter said, and they that
were with him, Master, the multitudes press thee and crush
thee,[8] and sayest thou, Who touched me ?[9]   But Jesus said,
Some one did touch me : for I perceived that power had
gone forth from me.[10]   And he looked round about to see
her that had done this thing.[11]   And when the woman saw
that she was not hid, she came trembling, and falling down

---

1. Matt. 9 : 18.
2. Mark 5 : 22.
3. Luke 8 : 41, 42.
4. Matt. 9 : 18.

5. Mark 5 : 23-27.
6. Luke 8 : 44.
7. Matt. 5 : 28-30.
8. Luke 8 : 45.

9. Mark 5 : 32.
10. Luke 8 : 46.
11. Mark 5 : 32.

before him declared in the presence of all the people for what cause she touched him, and how she was healed immediately.[1] But Jesus turning and seeing her, said, Daughter, be of good cheer ; thy faith hath made thee whole.[2] Go in peace, and be whole of thy plague.[3] And the woman was made whole from that hour.[4]

While he yet spake, there cometh one from the ruler of the synagogue's *house,* saying,[5] Thy daughter is dead : why troublest thou the Master any further? But Jesus, not heeding the word spoken, saith unto the ruler of the synagogue, Fear not, only believe,[6] and she shall be made whole.[7]

And they come to the house of the ruler of the synagogue ; and he beholdeth a tumult, and *many* weeping and wailing greatly.[8] And when he came to the house, he suffered not any man to enter in with him, save Peter, and John, and James, and the father of the maiden and her mother.[9] And when Jesus came into the ruler's house, and saw the flute-players, and the crowd making a tumult, he said,[10] Why make ye a tumult and weep?[11] Weep not.[12] Give place : for the damsel is not dead, but sleepeth. And they laughed him to scorn,[13] knowing that she was dead.[14] But he, having put them all forth, taketh the father of the child and her mother and them that were with him, and goeth in where the child was. And taking the child by the hand, he saith unto her, Talitha cumi ; which is, being interpreted, Damsel, I say unto thee, Arise.[15] And her spirit returned, and[16] straightway the damsel rose up, and walked ; for she was twelve years old. And they were amazed straightway with a great amazement. And he charged them much that no man should know this : and he commanded that *something* should be given her to eat.[17] And the fame hereof went forth into all that land.[18]

---

1. Luke 8 : 47.	7. Luke 8 : 40.	13. Matt. 9 : 24.
2. Matt. 9 : 22.	8. Mark 5 : 38.	14. Luke 8 : 53.
3. Mark 5 : 34.	9. Luke 8 : 51.	15. Mark 5 : 40, 41.
4. Matt. 9 : 22.	10. Matt. 9 : 23, 24.	16. Luke 8 : 55.
5. Luke 8 : 49.	11. Mark 5 : 39.	17. Mark 5 : 42.
6. Mark 5 : 35, 36.	12. Luke 8 : 52.	18. Matt. 9 : 26.

And as Jesus passed by from thence, two blind men followed him, crying out, and saying, Have mercy on us, thou son of David. And when he was come into the house, the blind men came to him : and Jesus saith unto them, Believe ye that I am able to do this? They say unto him, Yea, Lord. Then touched he their eyes, saying, According to your faith be it done unto you. And their eyes were opened. And Jesus strictly charged them, saying, See that no man know it. But they went forth, and spread abroad his fame in all that land.

And as they went forth, behold, there was brought to him a dumb man possessed with a devil. And when the devil was cast out, the dumb man spake : and the multitudes marvelled, saying, It was never so seen in Israel. But the Pharisees said, By the prince of the devils casteth he out devils.[1]

§ 48—JESUS SENDS FORTH THE TWELVE APOSTLES.

And he went out from thence and he cometh into his own country; and his disciples follow him. And when the sabbath was come, he began to teach in the synagogue : and many hearing him were astonished, saying, Whence hath this man these things? and, What is the wisdom that is given unto this man, and *what mean* such mighty works wrought by his hands? Is not this the carpenter, the son of Mary, the brother of James, and Joses, and Judas, and Simon? and are not his sisters here with us? And they were offended in him. And Jesus said unto them, A prophet is not without honour, save in his own country, and among his own kin, and in his own house. And he could there do no mighty work, save that he laid his hands upon a few sick folk, and healed them. And he marvelled because of their unbelief.[2]

And Jesus went about all the cities and the villages, teaching in their synagogues, and preaching the gospel of the kingdom, and healing all manner of disease and all

---

1. Matt. 9 : 27-34.   2. Mark 6 : 1-6.

manner of sickness. But when he saw the multitudes, he was moved with compassion for them, because they were distressed and scattered, as sheep not having a shepherd. Then saith he unto his disciples, The harvest truly is plenteous, but the labourers are few. Pray ye therefore the Lord of the harvest, that he send forth labourers into his harvest.[1]

Now the names of the twelve apostles are these: The first, Simon, who is called Peter, and Andrew his brother ; James the *son* of Zebedee, and John his brother ; Philip, and Bartholomew ; Thomas, and Matthew the publican ; James the *son* of Alphæus, and Thaddæus ; Simon the Canaæan, and Judas Iscariot, who also betrayed him. These twelve Jesus sent forth,[2] by two and two, and he gave them[3] power and authority over all devils, and to[4] heal all manner of disease and all manner of sickness.[5] And he sent them forth to preach the kingdom of God, and to heal the sick. And he[6] charged them, saying, Go not into *any* way of the Gentiles, and enter not into any city of the Samaritans : but go rather to the lost sheep of the house of Israel. And as ye go, preach, saying, The kingdom of heaven is at hand. Heal the sick, raise the dead, cleanse the lepers, cast out devils : freely ye received, freely give. Get you no gold, nor silver, nor brass in your purses ; no wallet for *your* journey, neither two coats, nor shoes, nor staff: for the labourer is worthy of his food. And into whatsoever city or village ye shall enter, search out who in it is worthy ; and there abide till ye go forth. And as ye enter into the house, salute it. And if the house be worthy, let your peace come upon it: but if it be not worthy, let your peace return to you. And whosoever shall not receive you, nor hear your words, as ye go forth out of that house or that city, shake off the dust of your feet[7] for a testimony unto them.[8] Verily I say unto you, It shall be more tolerable for the land of Sodom and Gomorrah in the day of judgement, than for that city.[9]

---

1. Matt. 9 : 35-38.
2. Matt. 10 : 2-5.
3. Mark 6 : 7.
4. Luke 9 : 1.
5. Matt. 10 : 1.
6. Luke 9 : 2, 3.
7. Matt. 10 : 5-14.
8. Mark 6 : 11.
9. Matt. 10 : 15.

Behold, I send you forth as sheep in the midst of wolves : be ye therefore wise as serpents, and harmless as doves. But beware of men : for they will deliver you up to councils, and in their synagogues they will scourge you ; yea and before governors and kings shall ye be brought for my sake, for a testimony to them and to the Gentiles. But when they deliver you up, be not anxious how or what ye shall speak : for it shall be given you in that hour what ye shall speak. For it is not ye that speak, but the Spirit of your Father that speaketh in you. And brother shall deliver up brother to death, and the father his child : and children shall rise up against parents, and cause them to be put to death. And ye shall be hated of all men for my name's sake : but he that endureth to the end, the same shall be saved. But when they persecute you in this city, flee into the next : for verily I say unto you, Ye shall not have gone through the cities of Israel, till the Son of man be come.

A disciple is not above his master, nor a servant above his lord. It is enough for the disciple that he be as his master, and the servant as his lord. If they have called the master of the house Beelzebub, how much more *shall they call* them of his household ! Fear them not therefore : for there is nothing covered, that shall not be revealed; and hid, that shall not be known. What I tell you in the darkness, speak ye in the light : and what ye hear in the ear, proclaim upon the housetops. And be not afraid of them which kill the body, but are not able to kill the soul : but rather fear him which is able to destroy both soul and body in hell. Are not two sparrows sold for a farthing? and not one of them shall fall on the ground without your Father : but the very hairs of your head are all numbered. Fear not therefore ; ye are of more value than many sparrows. Every one therefore who shall confess me before me, him will I also confess before my Father which is in heaven. But whosoever shall deny me before men, him will I also deny before my Father which is in heaven.

Think not that I came to send peace on the earth : I came[1]

---

1. Matt. 10 : 16-34.

not to send peace, but a sword. For I came to set a man at variance against his father, and the daughter against her mother, and the daughter in law against her mother in law : and a man's foes *shall be* they of his own household. He that loveth father or mother more than me is not worthy of me ; and he that loveth son or daughter more than me is not worthy of me. And he that doth not take his cross and follow after me, is not worthy of me. He that findeth his life shall lose it ; and he that loseth his life for my sake shall find it.

He that receiveth you receiveth me, and he that receiveth me receiveth him that sent me. He that receiveth a prophet in the name of a prophet shall receive a prophet's reward ; and he that receiveth a righteous man in the name of a righteous man shall receive a righteous man's reward. And whosoever shall give to drink unto one of these little ones a cup of cold water only, in the name of a disciple, verily I say unto you, he shall in no wise lose his reward.[1]

And it came to pass, when Jesus had made an end of commanding his twelve disciples, he departed thence to teach and preach in their cities.[2]

And they went out, and preached that *men* should repent. And they cast out many devils, and anointed with oil many that were sick, and healed them.[3]

§49—THE DEATH OF JOHN THE BAPTIST.

And when a convenient day was come, that Herod on his birthday made a supper to his lords, and the high captains, and the chief men of Galilee ; and when the daughter of Herodias herself came in and danced, she pleased Herod and them that sat at meat with him ; and the king said unto the damsel, Ask of me whatsoever thou wilt, and I will give it thee. And he sware unto her, Whatsoever thou shalt ask of me, I will give it thee, unto the half of my kingdom. And she went out, and said unto her mother, What shall I ask ? And she said, The head of John the Baptist. And she came in straightway with haste unto the king, and asked,

---

1. Matt. 10 : 34-42.   2. Matt. 11 : 1.   3. Mark 6 : 12, 13.

saying, I will that thou forthwith give me in a charger the head of John the Baptist And the king was exceeding sorry; but for the sake of his oaths, and of them that sat at meat, he would not reject her. And straightway the king sent forth a soldier of his guard, and commanded to bring his head : and he went and beheaded him in the prison, and brought his head in a charger, and gave it to the damsel ; and the damsel gave it to her mother. And when his disciples heard *thereof*, they came and took up his corpse, and laid it in a tomb,[1] and they went and told Jesus.[2]

Now Herod the tetrarch heard of all that was done : and he was much perplexed, because that it was said by some, that John was risen from the dead :[3] and therefore do these powers work in him ;[4] and by some, that Elijah had appeared ; and by others, that one of the old prophets was risen again. And Herod said, John I beheaded : but who is this, about whom I hear such things? And he sought to see him.[5]

§ 50—JESUS FEEDS FIVE THOUSAND BY A MIRACLE.

And the apostles gather themselves together unto Jesus; and they told him all things, whatsoever they had done, and whatsoever they had taught. And he saith unto them, Come ye yourselves apart into a desert place, and rest a while. For there were many coming and going, and they had no leisure so much as to eat. And they went away in the boat to a desert place apart[6] to the other side of the sea of Galilee, which is the sea of Tiberias.[7] And *the people* saw them going, and many knew *them*, and they ran there together on foot from all the cities, and outwent them. And he came forth and saw a great multitude,[8] and he welcomed them, and spake to them of the kingdom of God, and them that had need of healing he healed :[9] and he had compassion on them, because they were as sheep not having a shepherd : and he began to teach them many things.[10]

---

1. Mark 6 : 21-29.
2. Matt. 14 : 12.
3. Luke 9 : 7.
4. Mark 6 : 14, 15.
5. Luke 9 : 8, 9.
6. Mark 6 : 30-32.
7. John 6 : 1.
8. Mark 6 : 33, 34.
9. Luke 9 : 11.
10. Mark 6 : 34.

And Jesus went up into the mountain, and there he sat with his disciples. Now the passover, the feast of the Jews, was at hand. Jesus therefore lifting up his eyes, and seeing that a great multitude cometh unto him, saith unto Philip, Whence are we to buy bread, that these may eat ? And this he said to prove him : for he himself knew what he would do. Philip answered him, Two hundred pennyworth of bread is not sufficient for them, that every one may take a little.[1] And when the day was now far spent, his disciples came unto him, and said, The place is desert, and the day is now far spent: send them away, that they may go into the country and villages round about, and buy themselves somewhat to eat.[2] But Jesus said unto them, They have no need to go away ; give ye them to eat.[3] And they say unto him, Shall we go and buy two hundred pennyworth of bread, and give them to eat ? And he saith unto them, How many loaves have ye ? go and see.[4] One of his disciples, Andrew, Simon Peter's brother, saith unto him, There is a lad here, which hath five barley loaves, and two fishes : but what are these among so many ?[5] And he commanded them that all should sit down by companies upon the green grass. And they sat down in ranks, by hundreds, and by fifties. And he took the five loaves and the two fishes, and looking up to heaven, he blessed, and brake the loaves ; and he gave to the disciples to set before them ; and the two fishes divided he among them all. And they did all eat, and were filled.[6]

And when they were filled, he saith unto his disciples, Gather up the broken pieces which remain over, that nothing be lost. So they gathered them up, and filled twelve baskets with broken pieces from the five barley loaves, which remained over unto them that had eaten.[7] And they that ate the loaves were five thousand men,[8] besides women and children.[9] When therefore the people saw the sign which he did, they said, This is of a truth the prophet that cometh into the world.[10]

---

1. John 6 : 3-7.
2. Mark 6 : 35, 36.
3. Matt. 14 : 16.
4. Mark 6 : 37, 38.
5. John 6 : 8, 9.
6. Mark 6 : 39-42.
7. John 6 : 12, 13.
8. Mark 6 : 44.
9. Matt. 14 : 21.
10. John 6 : 14.

§ 51—JESUS WALKS UPON THE SEA.

And straightway he constrained his disciples to enter into the boat, and to go before *him* unto the other side to Bethsaida, while he himself sendeth the multitude away.[1]

Jesus therefore perceiving that they were about to come and take him by force, to make him king, withdrew again into the mountain himself alone[2] to pray.[3]

And when evening came, his disciples went down unto the sea; and they entered into a boat, and were going over the sea unto Capernaum. And it was now dark, and Jesus had not yet come to them. And the sea was rising by reason of a great wind that blew.[4] And when even was come, the boat was in the midst of the sea, and he alone on the land. And seeing them distressed in rowing, for the wind was contrary unto them, about the fourth watch of the night he cometh unto them, walking on the sea.[5] When therefore they had rowed about five and twenty or thirty furlongs, they behold Jesus walking on the sea, and drawing nigh unto the boat.[6] And he would have passed by them: but they, when they saw him walking on the sea, supposed that it was an apparition, and cried out: for they all saw him, and were troubled. But he straightway spake with them, and saith unto them, Be of good cheer: it is I; be not afraid.[7] And Peter answered him and said, Lord, if it be thou, bid me come unto thee upon the waters. And he said, Come. And Peter went down from the boat, and walked upon the waters, to come to Jesus. But when he saw the wind, he was afraid; and beginning to sink he cried out, saying, Lord, save me. And immediately Jesus stretched forth his hand, and took hold of him, and saith unto him, O thou of little faith, wherefore didst thou doubt? And when they were gone up into the boat, the wind ceased.[8] And they were sore amazed in themselves; for they understood not concerning the loaves, but their heart was hardened.[9] And straightway the boat

---

1. Mark 6: 45.
2. John 6: 15.
3. Matt. 14: 23.
4. John 6: 16-18.
5. Mark 6: 47, 48.
6. John 6: 19.
7. Mark 6: 48-50.
8. Matt. 14: 28-32.
9. Mark 6: 51, 52.

was at the land whither they were going.[1] And they that
were in the boat worshipped him, saying, Of a truth thou art
the Son of God.[2] And when they were come out of the
boat, straightway *the people* knew him, and ran round about
that whole region, and began to carry about on their beds
those that were sick, where they heard he was. And
wheresoever he entered, into villages, or into cities, or into
the country, they laid the sick in the marketplaces, and
besought him that they might touch if it were but the border
of his garment : and as many as touched him were made
whole.[3]

§ 52—JESUS DISCOURSES CONCERNING THE TRUE BREAD WHICH COMETH DOWN FROM HEAVEN.

On the morrow the multitude which stood on the other
side of the sea saw that there was none other boat there,
save one, and that Jesus entered not with his disciples into
the boat, but *that* his disciples went away alone (howbeit
there came boats from Tiberias nigh unto the place where
they ate the bread after the Lord had given thanks) : when
the multitude therefore saw that Jesus was not there,
neither his disciples, they themselves got into the boats, and
came to Capernaum, seeking Jesus. And when they found
him on the other side of the sea, they said unto him, Rabbi,
when camest thou hither ? Jesus answered them and said,
Verily, verily, I say unto you, Ye seek me, not because ye
saw signs, but because ye ate of the loaves, and were filled.
Work not for the meat which perisheth, but for the meat
which abideth unto eternal life, which the Son of man shall
give unto you : for him the Father, *even* God, hath sealed.
They said therefore unto him, What must we do, that we
may work the works of God ? Jesus answered and said unto
them, This is the work of God, that ye believe on him whom
he hath sent. They said therefore unto him, What then
doest thou for a sign, that we may see, and believe thee ?[4]

---

1. John 6: 21. 3. Mark 6 : 54-56. 4. John 6 : 22-30.
2. Matt. 14 : 33.

what workest thou ? Our fathers ate the manna in the
wilderness ; as it is written, He gave them bread out of
heaven to eat. Jesus therefore said unto them, Verily,
verily, I say unto you, It was not Moses that gave you the
bread out of heaven ; but my Father giveth you the true
bread out of heaven. For the bread of God is that which
cometh down out of heaven, and giveth life unto the world.
They said therefore unto him, Lord, evermore give us this
bread. Jesus said unto them, I am the bread of life : he
that cometh to me shall not hunger, and he that believeth
on me shall never thirst. But I said unto you, that ye have
seen me, and yet believe not. All that which the Father
giveth me shall come unto me ; and him that cometh to me
I will in no wise cast out. For I am come down from
heaven, not to do mine own will, but the will of him that
sent me. And this is the will of him that sent me, that of
all that which he hath given me I should lose nothing, but
should raise it up at the last day. For this is the will of my
Father, that every one that beholdeth the Son, and believeth
on him, should have eternal life ; and I will raise him up at
the last day.

The Jews therefore murmured concerning him, because he
said, I am the bread which came down out of heaven. And
they said, Is not this Jesus, the son of Joseph, whose
father and mother we know ? how doth he now say, I am
come down out of heaven ? Jesus answered and said unto
them, Murmur not among yourselves. No man can come to
me, except the Father which sent me draw him : and I will
raise him up in the last day. It is written in the prophets,
And they shall all be taught of God. Every one that hath
heard from the Father, and hath learned cometh unto me.
Not that any man hath seen the Father, save he which is
from God, he hath seen the Father. Verily, verily, I say
unto you, He that believeth hath eternal life. I am the
bread of life. Your fathers did eat the manna in the wilderness, and they died. This is the bread which cometh down
out of heaven, that a man may eat thereof, and not die. I[1]

---

1. John 6 : 31-50.

am the living bread which came down out of heaven : if any man eat of this bread, he shall live for ever : yea and the bread which I will give is my flesh, for the life of the world.

The Jews therefore strove one with another, saying, How can this man give us his flesh to eat? Jesus therefore said unto them, Verily, verily, I say unto you, Except ye eat the flesh of the Son of man and drink his blood, ye have not life in yourselves. He that eateth my flesh and drinketh my blood hath eternal life ; and I will raise him up at the last day. For my flesh is meat indeed, and my blood is drink indeed. He that eateth my flesh and drinketh my blood abideth in me, and I in him. As the living Father sent me, and I live because of the Father ; so he that eateth me, he also shall live because of me. This is the bread which came down out of heaven : not as the fathers did eat, and died : he that eateth this bread shall live for ever. These things said he in the synagogue, as he taught in Capernaum.

Many therefore of his disciples, when they heard *this*, said, This is a hard saying ; who can hear it? But Jesus knowing in himself that his disciples murmured at this, said unto them, Doth this cause you to stumble? *What* then if ye should behold the Son of man ascending where he was before? It is the spirit that quickeneth ; the flesh profiteth nothing : the words that I have spoken unto you are spirit, and are life: But there are some of you that believe not. For Jesus knew from the beginning who they were that believed not, and who it was that should betray him. And he said, For this cause have I said unto you, that no man can come unto me, except it be given unto him of the Father.

Upon this many of his disciples went back, and walked no more with him. Jesus said therefore unto the twelve, Would ye also go away? Simon Peter answered him, Lord, to whom shall we go? thou hast the words of eternal life. And we have believed and know that thou art the Holy One of God. Jesus answered them, Did not I choose you the twelve, and one of you is a devil? Now he spake of Judas *the son* of Simon Iscariot, for he it was that should betray him, *being* one of the twelve.[1]

---

1. John 6 : 51-71.

§ 53—JESUS TEACHES THE TRUE CAUSE OF
DEFILEMENT.

And after these things Jesus walked in Galilee: for he
would not walk in Judæa, because the Jews sought to kill
him.[1]

And there are gathered together unto him the Pharisees,
and certain of the scribes, which had come from Jerusalem,
and had seen that some of his disciples ate their bread with
defiled, that is, unwashen, hands. For the Pharisees, and
all the Jews, except they wash their hands diligently, eat
not, holding the tradition of the elders: and *when they come*
from the marketplace, except they wash themselves, they
eat not: and many other things there be, which they have
received to hold, washings of cups, and pots, and brasen
vessels. And the Pharisees and the scribes ask him, Why
walk not thy disciples according to the tradition of the
elders,[2] [for they wash not their hands when they eat
bread[3]], but eat their bread with defiled hands? And he
said unto them, Well did Isaiah prophesy of you hypocrites,
as it is written,

This people honoureth me with their lips,
But their heart is far from me.
But in vain do they worship me,
Teaching *as their* doctrines the precepts of men.

Ye leave the commandment of God, and hold fast the tradition of men. And he said unto them, Full well do ye reject
the commandment of God, that ye may keep your tradition.
For Moses said, Honour thy father and thy mother; and,
He that speaketh evil of father or mother, let him die the
death: but ye say, If a man shall say to his father or his
mother, That wherewith thou mightest have been profited
by me is Corban, that is to say, Given *to God;* ye no longer
suffer him to do aught for his father or his mother; making
void the word of God by your tradition, which ye have
delivered: and many such like things ye do. And he called

---

1. John 7 : 1.　　　2. Mark 7 : 1-5.　　　3. Matt. 15 : 2.

to him the multitude again, and said unto them, Hear me all of you, and understand: there is nothing from without the man, that going into him can defile him: but the things which proceed out of the man are those that defile the man. And when he was entered into the house from the multitude, his disciples asked of him the parable,[1] and said unto him, Knowest thou that the Pharisees were offended, when they heard this saying? But he answered and said, Every plant which my heavenly Father planted not, shall be rooted up. Let them alone: they are blind guides And if the blind guide the blind, both shall fall into a pit. And Peter answered and said unto him, Declare unto us the parable. And he said, Are ye also even yet without understanding?[2] Perceive not that whatsoever from without goeth into the man, *it* cannot defile him; because it goeth not into his heart, but into his belly, and goeth out into the draught? *This he said*, making all meats clean. And he said, That which proceedeth out of the man, that defileth the man. For from within, out of the heart of men, evil thoughts proceed, fornications, thefts, murders, adulteries, covetings, wickednesses, deceit, lasciviousness, an evil eye, railing, pride, foolishness: all these evil things proceed from within, and defile the man;[3] but to eat with unwashen hands defileth not the man.[4]

§ 54—JESUS HEALS THE DAUGHTER OF A SYRO-PHŒNICIAN WOMAN, AND WORKS OTHER MIRACLES.

And Jesus went out thence, and withdrew into the parts of Tyre and Sidon.[5] And he entered into a house, and would have no man know it: and he could not be hid. But straightway a woman, whose little daughter had an unclean spirit, having heard of him, came and fell down at his feet. Now the woman was a Greek, a Syrophœnician by race. And she besought him that he would cast forth the devil out of her daughter,[6] and cried, saying, Have mercy on me,

---

1. Mark 7 : 14-17. 3. Mark 7 : 18-23. 5. Matt. 15 : 21.
2. Matt. 15 ; 12-16. 4. Matt. 15 : 20. 6. Mark 7 : 21-26.

6

O Lord, thou son of David; my daughter is grievously vexed
with a devil. But he answered her not a word. And his
disciples came and besought him, saying, Send her away;
for she crieth after us. But he answered and said, I was not
sent but unto the lost sheep of the house of Israel. But she
came and worshipped him, saying, Lord, help me. And he
answered and said[1] unto her, Let the children first be filled:
for it is not meet to take the children's bread and cast it to
the dogs.[2] But she said, Yea, Lord: for even the dogs eat
of the crumbs which fall from their masters' table. Then
Jesus answered and said unto her, O woman, great is thy
faith: be it done unto thee even as thou wilt.[3] For this
saying go thy way; the devil is gone out of thy daughter.
And she went away unto her house, and found the child laid
upon the bed, and the devil gone out.

And again he went out from the borders of Tyre, and
came through Sidon unto the sea of Galilee, through the
midst of the borders of Decapolis,[4] and he went up into
the mountain and sat there.[5] And they bring unto him one
that was deaf, and had an impediment in his speech; and
they beseech him to lay his hand upon him. And he took
him aside from the multitude privately, and put his fingers
into his ears, and he spat, and touched his tongue; and
looking up to heaven, he sighed, and saith unto him, Eph-
phatha, that is, Be opened. And his ears were opened, and
the bond of his tongue was loosed, and he spake plain.
And he charged them that they should tell no man: but the
more he charged them, so much the more a great deal they
published it. And they were beyond measure astonished,
saying, He hath done all things well: he maketh even the
deaf to hear, and the dumb to speak.[6]

And there came unto him great multitudes, having with
them the lame, blind, dumb, maimed, and many others, and
they cast them down at his feet; and he healed them: insomuch that the multitude wondered, when they saw the
dumb speaking, the maimed whole, and the lame walking,
and the blind seeing: and they glorified the God of Israel.[7]

1. Matt. 15 : 22-26.   4. Mark 7 : 29-31.   6. Mark 7 : 32-37.
2. Mark 7 : 27.   5. Matt. 15 : 29.   7. Matt. 15 : 30, 31.
3. Matt. 15 : 27, 28.

§ 55—JESUS FEEDS THE FOUR THOUSAND.

In those days, when there was again a great multitude, and they had nothing to eat, he called unto him his disciples, and saith unto them, I have compassion on the multitude, because they continue with me now three days, and have nothing to eat: and if I send them away fasting to their home, they will faint in the way; and some of them are come from far. And his disciples answered him, Whence shall one be able to fill[1] so great a multitude[2] with bread here in a desert place?[3] And Jesus saith unto them, How many loaves have ye? And they said, Seven, and a few small fishes. And he commanded the multitude to sit down on the ground; and he took the seven loaves and the fishes; and he gave thanks and brake, and gave to the disciples, and the disciples to the multitudes.[4] [And they had a few small fishes: and having blessed them, he commanded to set these also before them.] And they did eat, and were filled: and they took up, of broken pieces that remained over, seven baskets[5] full. And they that did eat were four thousand men, beside women and children. And he sent away the multitudes, and entered into the boat, and came into the borders of Magadan[6] [and] Dalmanutha.[7]

§ 56—JESUS WARNS HIS DISCIPLES AGAINST THE
LEAVEN OF THE PHARISEES.

And the Pharisees and Sadducees came, and[8] began to question with him,[9] and tempting him, asked him to shew them a sign from heaven.[10] And he sighed deeply in his spirit,[11] and said unto them, When it is evening, ye say, *It will be* fair weather: for the heaven is red. And in the morning, *It will be* foul weather to-day : for the heaven is red and lowring. Ye know how to discern the face of the heaven ; but

---

1. Mark 8 : 1-4.	5. Mark 8 : 7, 8.	9. Mark 8 : 11.
2. Matt. 15 : 33.	6. Matt. 15 : 38, 39.	10. Matt. 16 : 1.
3. Mark 8 : 4.	7. Mark 8 : 10.	11. Mark 8 : 12.
4. Matt. 15 : 34-36.	8. Matt. 16 : 1.	

ye cannot *discern* the signs of the times.　An evil and adulterous generation seeketh after a sign ;[1] verily I say unto you,[2] There shall no sign be given unto it but the sign of Jonah.[3]　And he left them, and again entering into *the boat* departed to the other side.[4]

And the disciples[5] forgot to take bread; and they had not in the boat with them more than one loaf.[6]　And Jesus said unto them, Take heed and beware of the leaven of the Pharisees and Sadducees,[7] and the leaven of Herod.　And they reasoned one with another, saying, We have no bread. And Jesus perceiving it saith unto them,[8] O ye of little faith,[9] why reason ye, because ye have no bread? do ye not yet perceive, neither understand? have ye your heart hardened?　Having eyes, see ye not? and having ears, hear ye not? and do ye not remember?　When I brake the five loaves among the five thousand, how many baskets full of broken pieces took ye up?　They say unto him, Twelve. And when the seven[10] loaves[11] among the four thousand, how many basketfuls of broken pieces took ye up?　And they say unto him, Seven.　And he said unto them,[12] How is it that ye do not perceive that I spake not to you concerning bread? But beware of the leaven of the Pharisees and Sadducees. Then understood they how that he bade them not beware of the leaven of bread, but of the teaching of the Pharisees and Sadducees.[13]

§ 57—JESUS HEALS A BLIND MAN.

And they come unto Bethsaida.　And they bring to him a blind man, and beseech him to touch him.　And he took hold of the blind man by the hand, and brought him out of the village ; and when he had spit on his eyes, and laid his hands upon him, he asked him, Seest thou aught?　And he looked up, and said, I see men ; for I behold *them* as trees,

---

1. Matt. 16 : 2-4.
2. Mark 8 : 12.
3. Matt. 16 : 4.
4. Mark 8 : 13.
5. Matt. 16 : 5.

6. Mark 8 : 14.
7. Matt. 16 : 6.
8. Mark 8 : 15-17.
9. Matt. 14 : 8.

10. Mark 8 : 17-20.
11. Matt. 16 : 10.
12. Mark 8 : 20, 21.
13. Matt. 16 : 11, 12.

walking. Then again he laid his hands upon his eyes ; and he looked stedfastly, and was restored, and saw all things clearly. And he sent him away to his home, saying, Do not even enter into the village.[1]

§ 58—JESUS FORETELLS HIS ATONEMENT AND EXALTATION.

And Jesus went forth, and his disciples, into the villages of Cæsarea Philippi.[2] And it came to pass, as he was praying alone, the disciples were with him : and he asked them, saying, Who do the multitudes say that I am ? And they answering said,[3] Some *say* John the Baptist ; some, Elijah : and others, Jeremiah, or[4] that one of the old prophets is risen again. And he said unto them, But who say ye that I am ?[5] And Simon Peter answered and said, Thou art the Christ, the Son of the living God. And Jesus answered and said unto him, Blessed art thou, Simon Bar-Jonah : for flesh and blood hath not revealed it unto thee, but my Father which is in heaven. And I also say unto thee, that thou art Peter, and upon this rock I will build my church ; and the gates of Hades shall not prevail against it. I will give unto thee the keys of the kingdom of heaven : and whatsoever thou shalt bind on earth shall be bound in heaven : and whatsoever thou shalt loose on earth shall be loosed in heaven. Then charged he the disciples that they should tell no man that he was the Christ.

From that time began Jesus to shew unto his disciples, how that he must go unto Jerusalem, and suffer many things,[6] and be rejected by the elders, and the chief priests, and the scribes, and be killed, and after three days rise again. And he spake the saying openly. And Peter took him, and began to rebuke him,[7] saying, Be it far from thee, Lord : this shall never be unto thee. But he turned, and said unto Peter, Get thee behind me, Satan : thou art a

---

1. Mark 8 : 22-26.
2. Mark 8 : 27.
3. Luke 9 : 18, 19.

4. Matt. 16 : 14.
5. Luke 9 : 19, 20.

6. Matt. 16 : 16-21.
7. Mark 8 : 31, 32.

stumblingblock unto me : for thou mindest not the things of God, but the things of men.[1]

And he called unto him the multitude with his disciples, and said unto them, If any man would come after me, let him deny himself, and take up his cross[2] daily,[3] and follow me. For whosoever would save his life shall lose it ; and whosoever shall lose his life for my sake and the gospel's shall save it. For what doth it profit a man, to gain the whole world, and forfeit his life ? For what should a man give in exchange for his life ? For whosoever shall be ashamed of me and of my words in this adulterous and sinful generation, the Son of man also shall be ashamed of him, when he cometh in the glory of his Father with the holy angels,[4] and then shall he render unto every man according to his deeds. Verily I say unto you, There be some of them that stand here, which shall in no wise taste of death, till they see the Son of man coming in his kingdom[5] [till they see the kingdom of God come with power[6]].

§ 59—THE TRANSFIGURATION.

And it came to pass about eight days after these sayings, he took with him Peter and John and James, and went up into[7] a high mountain apart by themselves,[8] to pray,[9] and he was transfigured before them.[10] And as he was praying, the fashion of his countenance was altered,[11] and his face did shine as the sun,[12] and his garments became glistering, exceeding white ; so as no fuller on earth can whiten them.[13] And behold, there talked with him two men, which were Moses and Elijah ; who appeared in glory, and spake of his decease which he was about to accomplish at Jerusalem. Now Peter and they that were with him were heavy with sleep : but when they were fully awake, they saw his glory, and the two men that stood with him. And it came

---

1. Matt. 16 : 22, 23.	6. Mark 9 : 1.	10. Mark 9 : 2.
2. Mark 8 : 34.	7. Luke 9 : 28.	11. Luke 9 : 29.
3. Luke 9 : 23.	8. Mark 9 : 2.	12. Matt. 17 : 2.
4. Mark 8 : 34-38.	9. Luke 9 : 28.	13. Mark 9 : 3.
5. Matt. 16 : 27, 28.		

to pass, as they were parting from him, Peter said unto Jesus, Master, it is good for us to be here : and let us make three tabernacles ; one for thee, and one for Moses, and one for Elijah : not knowing what he said.[1] While he was yet speaking, behold, a bright cloud overshadowed them :[2] and they feared as they entered into the cloud :[3] and behold a voice out of the cloud, saying, This is my beloved Son, in whom I am well pleased ; hear ye him. And when the disciples heard it, they fell on their face, and were sore afraid. And Jesus came and touched them and said, Arise, and be not afraid.[4] And suddenly looking round about, they saw no one any more, save Jesus only with themselves.

And as they were coming down from the mountain, he charged them that they should tell no man what things they had seen, save when the Son of man should have risen again from the dead. And they kept the saying, questioning among themselves what the rising again from the dead should mean. And they asked him, saying, The scribes say that Elijah must first come. And he said unto them, Elijah indeed cometh first, and restoreth all things : and how is it written of the Son of man, that he should suffer many things and be set at nought ?[5] But I say unto you, that Elijah is come already, and they knew him not, but did unto him whatsoever they listed,[6] even as it is written of him.[7] Even so shall the Son of man also suffer of them. Then understood the disciples that he spake unto them of John the Baptist.[8] And they held their peace, and told no man in those days any of the things which they had seen.[9]

---

1. Luke 9 : 30-33.	4. Matt. 17 : 5-7.	7. Mark 9 : 13.
2. Matt. 17 : 5.	5. Mark 9 : 8-12.	8. Matt. 17 : 12, 13.
3. Luke 9 : 34.	6. Matt. 17 : 12.	9. Luke 8 : 36.

§ 60—JESUS CASTS A DUMB AND DEAF SPIRIT
OUT OF A CHILD.

And it came to pass, on the next day, when they were
come down from the mountain,[1] when they came to the
disciples, they saw a great multitude about them, and scribes
questioning with them. And straightway all the multitude,
when they saw him, were greatly amazed, and running to
him saluted him. And he asked them, What question ye
with them? And one of the multitude answered him,[2]
Master, I beseech thee to look upon my son; for he is mine
only child :[3] [for he is epileptic, and suffereth grievously :
for oft-times he falleth into the fire, and oft-times into the
water,[4]] which hath a dumb spirit; and wheresoever it taketh
him, it dasheth him down : and he foameth, and grindeth
his teeth, and pineth away :[5] and it hardly departeth from
him, bruising him sorely. And I besought thy disciples,[6]
that they should cast it out; and they were not able. And
he answereth them and saith, O faithless generation, how
long shall I be with you? how long shall I bear with you?
bring him unto me. And they brought him unto him : and
when he saw him, straightway the spirit tare him grievously;
and he fell on the ground, and wallowed foaming. And he
asked his father, How long time is it since this hath come
unto him? And he said, From a child. And oft-times it
hath cast him both into the fire and into the waters, to
destroy him : but if thou canst do anything, have compassion on us, and help us. And Jesus said unto him, If thou
canst! All things are possible to him that believeth.
Straightway the father of the child cried out, and said, I
believe; help thou mine unbelief. And when Jesus saw
that a multitude came running together, he rebuked the unclean spirit, saying unto him, Thou dumb and deaf spirit, I
command thee, come out of him, and enter no more into
him. And having cried out, and torn him much, he came

---

1. Luke 9 : 37.
2. Mark 9 : 14-17.
3. Luke 9 : 38.
4. Matt. 17 : 15.
5. Mark 9 : 17, 18.
6. Luke 9 : 39.

out : and *the child* became as one dead ; insomuch that the more part said, He is dead.[1] But Jesus rebuked the unclean spirit and healed the boy, and[2] took him by the hand and raised him up ; and he arose,[3] and [Jesus] gave him back to his father, and they were all astonished at the majesty of God.[4] And when he was come into the house, his disciples asked him privately, *saying*, We could not cast it out. And he said unto them, This kind can come out by nothing, save by prayer.[5]

[Then came the disciples to Jesus apart, and said, Why could we not cast it out ? And he saith unto them, Because of your little faith : for verily I say unto you, If ye have faith as a grain of mustard seed, ye shall say unto this mountain, Remove hence to yonder place ; and it shall remove ; and nothing shall be impossible unto you.[6]]

§ 61—JESUS FORETELLS HIS DEATH, PAYS THE TRI-BUTE MONEY, AND TEACHES HUMILITY, FOR-BEARANCE AND BROTHERLY LOVE.

And they went forth from thence, and passed through Galilee ; and he would not that any man should know it.[7]

But while all were marvelling at all the things which he did, he said unto his disciples, Let these words sink into your ears :[8] The Son of man is delivered up into the hands of men, and they shall kill him ; and when he is killed, after three days he shall rise again.[9] And they were exceeding sorry.[10]

But they understood not this saying, and it was concealed from them, that they should not perceive it : and they were afraid to ask him about this saying.[11] And they came to Capernaum.[12]

And when they were come to Capernaum, they that received the half-shekel came to Peter, and said, Doth not your master pay the half-shekel ? He saith, Yea. And

---

1. Mark 9: 18-26.
2. Luke 9: 42.
3. Mark 9: 27.
4. Luke 9: 42, 43.
5. Mark 9: 28, 29.
6. Matt. 17: 19, 20.
7. Mark 9: 30.
8. Luke 9: 43, 44.
9. Mark 9: 31.
10. Matt. 17: 23.
11. Luke 9: 45.
12. Mark 9: 33.

when he came into the house, Jesus spake first to him, saying, What thinkest thou, Simon? the kings of the earth, from whom do they receive toll or tribute? from their sons, or from strangers? And when he said, From strangers, Jesus said unto him, Therefore the sons are free. But, lest we cause them to stumble, go thou to the sea, and cast a hook, and take up the fish that first cometh up; and when thou hast opened his mouth, thou shalt find a shekel: that take, and give unto them for me and thee.[1]

And there arose a reasoning among them, which of them should be greatest,[2] and when he was in the house he asked them, What were ye reasoning in the way? But they held their peace: for they had disputed one with another in the way, who *was* the greatest. And he sat down, and called the twelve; and he saith unto them, If any man would be first, he shall be last of all, and minister of all. And he took a little child, and set him in the midst of them: and taking him in his arms, he said unto them,[3] Verily I say unto you, Except ye turn, and become as little children, ye shall in no wise enter into the kingdom of heaven. Whosoever therefore shall humble himself as this little child, the same is the greatest in the kingdom of heaven. And whoso shall receive one such little child in my name receiveth me,[4] and whosoever receiveth me, receiveth not me, but him that sent me,[5] for he that is least among you all, the same is great.[6]

John said unto him, Master, we saw one casting out devils in thy name: and we forbade him, because he followed not us. But Jesus said, Forbid him not: for there is no man which shall do a mighty work in my name, and be able quickly to speak evil of me. For he that is not against us is for us. For whosoever shall give you a cup of water to drink, because ye are Christ's, verily I say unto you, he shall in no wise lose his reward. And whosoever shall cause one of these little ones that believe on me to stumble, it were better for him if a great millstone were hanged about his neck,[7] and *that* he should be sunk in the depth of the

---

1. Matt. 17 : 24-27.   4. Matt. 18 : 3-5.   6. Luke 9 : 48.
2. Luke 9 : 46.   5. Mark 8 : 37.   7. Mark 9 : 38-42.
3. Mark 9 : 33-36.

sea. Woe unto the world because of occasions of stumbling ! for it must needs be that the occasions come ; but woe to that man through whom the occasion cometh ! And if thy hand or thy foot causeth thee to stumble, cut it off, and cast it from thee : it is good for thee to enter into life maimed or halt, rather than having two hands or two feet to be cast into the eternal fire.[1] And if thy foot cause thee to stumble, cut it off : it is good for thee to enter into life halt, rather than having thy two feet to be cast into hell. And if thine eye cause thee to stumble,[2] pluck it out and cast it from thee :[3] it is good for thee to enter into the kingdom of God with one eye, rather than having two eyes to be cast into hell ; where their worm dieth not, and the fire is not quenched. For every one shall be salted with fire. Salt is good : but if the salt have lost its saltness, wherewith will ye season it ? Have salt in yourselves, and be at peace one with another.[4]

See that ye despise not one of these little ones ; for I say unto you, that in heaven their angels do always behold the face of my Father which is in heaven. How think ye ? if any man have a hundred sheep, and one of them be gone astray, doth he not leave the ninety and nine, and go unto the mountains, and seek that which goeth astray ? And if so be that he find it, verily I say unto you, he rejoiceth over it more than over the ninety and nine which have not gone astray. Even so it is not the will of your Father which is in heaven, that one of these little ones should perish.

And if thy brother sin against thee, go, shew him his fault between thee and him alone : if he hear thee, thou hast gained thy brother. But if he hear *thee* not, take with thee one or two more, that at the mouth of two witnesses or three every word may be established. And if he refuse to hear them, tell it unto the church ; and if he refuse to hear the church also, let him be unto thee as the Gentile and the publican. Verily I say unto you, What things soever ye shall bind on earth shall be bound in heaven : and what things soever ye shall loose on earth shall be loosed in heaven. Again I say unto you, that if two of you shall

---

1. Matt. 18 : 6-8.   3. Matt. 18: 9.   4. Mark 9 : 47-50.
2. Mark 9 : 45-47.

agree on earth as touching anything that they shall ask, it
shall be done for them of my Father which is in heaven.
For where two or three are gathered together in my name,
there am I in the midst of them.[1]

§ 62—THE PARABLE OF THE KING AND HIS
SERVANTS.

Then came Peter, and said to him, Lord, how oft shall my
brother sin against me, and I forgive him? until seven
times? Jesus saith unto him, I say not unto thee, Until
seven times; but, Until seventy times seven. Therefore is
the kingdom of heaven likened unto a certain king, which
would make a reckoning with his servants. And when he
had begun to reckon, one was brought unto him, which
owed him ten thousand talents. But forasmuch as he had
not *wherewith* to pay, his lord commanded him to be sold,
and his wife, and children, and all that he had, and payment
to be made. The servant therefore fell down and worshipped
him, saying, Lord, have patience with me, and I will pay
thee all. And the lord of that servant, being moved with
compassion, released him, and forgave him the debt. But
that servant went out, and found one of his fellow-servants,
which owed him a hundred pence: and he laid hold on him,
and took *him* by the throat, saying, Pay what thou owest.
So his fellow-servant fell down and besought him, saying,
Have patience with me, and I will pay thee. And he would
not: but went and cast him into prison, till he should pay
that which was due. So when his fellow-servants saw what
was done, they were exceeding sorry, and came and told unto
their lord all that was done. Then his lord called him unto
him, and saith to him, Thou wicked servant, I forgave thee
all that debt, because thou besoughtest me: shouldest not
thou also have had mercy on thy fellow-servant, even as I
had mercy on thee? And his lord was wroth, and delivered
him to the tormentors, till he should pay all that was due.
So shall also my heavenly Father do unto you, if ye forgive
not everyone his brother from your hearts.[2]

---

1. Matt. 18: 10-20.   2. Matt. 18: 21-35.

§ 63—JESUS TEACHES PUBLICLY IN THE TEMPLE.

[And after these things Jesus walked in Galilee : for he would not walk in Judæa, because the Jews sought to kill him.]

Now the feast of the Jews, the feast of tabernacles, was at hand. His brethren therefore said unto him, Depart hence, and go into Judæa, that thy disciples also may behold thy works which thou doest. For no man doeth anything in secret, and himself seeketh to be known openly. If thou doest these things, manifest thyself to the world. For even his brethren did not believe on him. Jesus therefore saith unto them, My time is not yet come ; but your time is alway ready. The world cannot hate you ; but me it hateth, because I testify of it, that its works are evil. Go ye up unto the feast: I go not up yet unto this feast ; because my time is not yet fulfilled. And having said these things unto them, he abode *still* in Galilee.

But when his brethren were gone up unto the feast, then went he also up, not publicly, but as it were in secret. The Jews therefore sought him at the feast, and said, Where is he ? And there was much murmuring among the multitudes concerning him : some said, He is a good man ; others said, Not so, but he leadeth the multitude astray. Howbeit no man spake openly of him for fear of the Jews.

But when it was now the midst of the feast Jesus went up into the temple, and taught. The Jews therefore marvelled, saying, How knoweth this man letters, having never learned? Jesus therefore answered them, and said, My teaching is not mine, but his that sent me. If any man willeth to do his will, he shall know of the teaching, whether it be of God, or *whether* I speak from myself. He that speaketh from himself, seeketh his own glory : but he that seeketh the glory of him that sent him, the same is true, and no unrighteousness is in him. Did not Moses give you the law, and *yet* none of you doeth the law ? Why seek ye to kill me ? The multitude answered, Thou hast a devil : who seeketh to kill[1]

---

1. John 7: 1-20.

thee? Jesus answered and said unto them, I did one work, and ye all marvel. For this cause hath Moses given you circumcision (not that it is of Moses, but of the fathers); and on the sabbath ye circumcise a man. If a man receiveth circumcision on the sabbath, that the law of Moses may not be broken; are ye wroth with me, because I made a man every whit whole on the sabbath? Judge not according to appearance, but judge righteous judgement.

Some therefore of them of Jerusalem said, Is not this he whom they seek to kill? And lo, he speaketh openly, and they say nothing unto him. Can it be that the rulers indeed know that this is the Christ? Howbeit we know this man whence he is: but when the Christ cometh, no one knoweth whence he is. Jesus therefore cried in the temple, teaching and saying, Ye both know me, and know whence I am; and I am not come of myself, but he that sent me is true, whom ye know not. I know him; because I am from him, and he sent me. They sought therefore to take him: and no man laid his hand on him, because his hour was not yet come. But of the multitude many believed on him; and they said, When the Christ shall come, will he do more signs than those which this man hath done? The Pharisees heard the multitude murmuring these things concerning him; and the chief priests and Pharisees sent officers to take him. Jesus therefore said, Yet a little while am I with you, and I go unto him that sent me. Ye shall seek me, and shall not find me: and where I am, ye cannot come. The Jews therefore said among themselves, Whither will this man go that we shall not find him? will he go unto the Dispersion among the Greeks, and teach the Greeks? What is this word that he said, Ye shall seek me, and shall not find me: and where I am, ye cannot come?

Now on the last day, the great *day* of the feast, Jesus stood and cried, saying, If any man thirst, let him come unto me, and drink. He that believeth on me, as the Scripture hath said, out of his belly shall flow rivers of living water. But this spake he of the Spirit, which they that[1]

---

1. John 7: 21-39.

believed on him were to receive ; for the Spirit was not yet
given ; because Jesus was not yet glorified. *Some* of the multitude therefore, when they heard these words, said, This is
of a truth the prophet. Others said, This is the Christ.
But some said, What, doth the Christ come out of Galilee ?
Hath not the scripture said that the Christ cometh of the
seed of David, and from Bethlehem, the village where
David was ? So there arose a division in the multitude
because of him. And some of them would have taken him ;
but no man laid hands on him.

The officers therefore came to the chief priests and Pharisees ; and they said unto them, Why did ye not bring him?
The officers answered, Never man so spake. The Pharisees
therefore answered them, Are ye also led astray? Hath any
of the rulers believed on him, or of the Pharisees? But
this multitude which knoweth not the law are accursed.
Nicodemus saith unto them (he that came to him before,
being one of them), Doth our law judge a man, except it
first hear from himself and know what he doeth? They
answered and said unto him, Art thou also of Galilee?
Search, and see that out of Galilee ariseth no prophet.

[And they went every man unto his own house :[1] but
Jesus went unto the mount of Olives.[2]

§ 64—THE WOMAN TAKEN IN ADULTERY BROUGHT TO JESUS.[*]

And early in the morning he came again into the temple,
and all the people came unto him : and he sat down, and
taught them. And the scribes and the Pharisees bring a
woman taken in adultery ; and having set her in the midst,
they say unto him, Master, this woman hath been taken in
adultery, in the very act. Now in the law Moses commanded
us to stone such : what then sayst thou of her? And this
they said, tempting him, that they might have *whereof* to
accuse him. But Jesus stooped down, and with his finger

---

1. John 7 : 40-53.   2. John 8 : 1.
[*] John 7 : 53 to John 8 : 11 is omitted in most ancient versions.

wrote on the ground. But when they continued asking
him, he lifted up himself, and said unto them, He that is
without sin among you, let him first cast a stone at her.
And again he stooped down, and with his finger wrote on
the ground.   And they, when they heard it, went out one
by one, beginning from the eldest, *even* unto the last: and
Jesus was left alone, and the woman, where she was, in the
midst.   And Jesus lifted up himself, and said unto her,
Woman, where are they ? did no man condemn thee ?   And
she said, No man, Lord.   And Jesus said, Neither do I
condemn thee: go thy way: from henceforth sin no more.[1]]

§ 65—JESUS PROCLAIMS HIMSELF THE SON OF GOD
AND REBUKES THE UNBELIEVING JEWS.

Again therefore Jesus spake unto them, saying, I am the
light of the world : he that followeth me shall not walk in
the darkness, but shall have the light of life.   The Pharisees
therefore said unto him, Thou bearest witness of thyself ;
thy witness is not true. Jesus answered and said unto
them, Even if I bear witness of myself, my witness is true ;
for I know whence I came, and whither I go ; but ye know
not whence I come, or whither I go.   Ye judge after the
flesh ; I judge no man.   Yea and if I judge, my judgement
is true; for I am not alone, but I and the Father that sent
me.   Yea and in your law it is written, that the witness of
two men is true.   I am he that beareth witness of myself,
and the Father that sent me beareth witness of me.   They
said therefore unto him, Where is thy Father ? Jesus
answered, Ye know neither me, nor my Father : if ye knew
me, ye would know my Father also.   These words spake he
in the treasury, as he taught in the temple : and no man
took him ; because his hour was not yet come.

He said therefore again unto them, I go away, and ye shall
seek me, and shall die in your sin : whither I go, ye cannot
come.   The Jews therefore said, Will he kill himself, that[2]

---

1. John 8: 2-11.   2. John 8 : 12-22.

he saith, Whither I go, ye cannot come? And he said unto
them, Ye are from beneath; I am from above: ye are of
this world; I am not of this world. I said therefore unto
you, that ye shall die in your sins: for except ye believe
that I am *he*, ye shall die in your sins. They said therefore
unto him, Who art thou? Jesus said unto them, Even that
which I have also spoken unto you from the beginning. I
have many things to speak and to judge concerning you:
howbeit he that sent me is true; and the things which I
heard from him, these speak I unto the world. They perceived not that he spake to them of the Father. Jesus
therefore said, When ye have lifted up the Son of man, then
shall ye know that I am *he*, and *that* I do nothing of myself,
but as the Father taught me, I speak these things. And he
that sent me is with me; he hath not left me alone; for I
do always the things that are pleasing to him. As he spake
these things, many believed on him.

Jesus therefore said to those Jews which had believed
him, If ye abide in my word, *then* are ye truly my disciples;
and ye shall know the truth, and the truth shall make you
free. They answered unto him, We be Abraham's seed,
and have never yet been in bondage to any man: how sayest
thou, Ye shall be made free? Jesus answered them, Verily,
verily, I say unto you, Every one that committeth sin is the
bondservant of sin. And the bondservant abideth not in
the house for ever: the son abideth for ever. If therefore
the Son shall make you free, ye shall be free indeed. I
know that ye are Abraham's seed; yet ye seek to kill me,
because my word hath not free course in you. I speak
the things which I have seen with *my* Father: and ye also
do the things which ye heard from *your* father. They
answered and said unto him, Our father is Abraham.
Jesus saith unto them, If ye were Abraham's children, ye
would do the works of Abraham. But now ye seek to kill
me, a man that hath told you the truth, which I heard from
God: this did not Abraham. Ye do the works of your
father.[1] They said unto him, We were not born of fornica-

---

1. John 8: 22-41.

tion; we have one Father, *even* God. Jesus said unto them, If God were your Father, ye would love me: for I came forth and am come from God; for neither have I come of myself, but he sent me. Why do ye not understand my speech? *Even* because ye cannot hear my word. Ye are of *your* father the devil, and the lusts of your father it is your will to do. He was a murderer from the beginning, and stood not in the truth, because there is no truth in him. When he speaketh a lie, he speaketh of his own: for he is a liar, and the father thereof. But because I say the truth, ye believe me not. Which of you convicteth me of sin? If I say truth, why do ye not believe me? He that is of God heareth the words of God: for this cause ye hear *them* not, because ye are not of God. The Jews answered and said unto him, Say we not well that thou art a Samaritan, and hast a devil? Jesus answered, I have not a devil; but I honour my Father, and ye dishonour me. But I seek not mine own glory: there is one that seeketh and judgeth. Verily, verily, I say unto you, If a man keep my word, he shall never see death. The Jews said unto him, Now we know that thou hast a devil. Abraham is dead, and the prophets; and thou sayest, If a man keep my word, he shall never taste of death. Art thou greater than our father Abraham, which is dead? and the prophets are dead: whom makest thou thyself? Jesus answered, If I glorify myself, my glory is nothing: it is my Father that glorifieth me; of whom ye say, that he is your God; and ye have not known him: but I know him; and if I should say, I know him not, I shall be like unto you, a liar: but I know him, and keep his word. Your father Abraham rejoiced to see my day; and he saw it, and was glad. The Jews therefore said unto him, Thou art not yet fifty years old, and hast thou seen Abraham? Jesus said unto them, Verily, verily, I say unto you, Before Abraham was, I am. They took up stones therefore to cast at him: but Jesus hid himself, and went out of the temple.[1]

---

1. John 8: 41-59.

§ 66—JESUS GIVES SIGHT TO A MAN BORN BLIND.

And as he passed by, he saw a man blind from his birth. And his disciples asked him, saying, Rabbi, who did sin, this man, or his parents, that he should be born blind? Jesus answered, Neither did this man sin, nor his parents: but that the works of God should be made manifest in him. We must work the works of him that sent me, while it is day : the night cometh, when no man can work. When I am in the world, I am the light of the world. When he had thus spoken, he spat on the ground, and made clay of the spittle, and anointed his eyes with the clay, and said unto him, Go, wash in the pool of Siloam (which is by interpretation, Sent). He went away therefore, and washed, and came seeing. The neighbours therefore, and they which saw him aforetime, that he was a beggar, said, Is not this he that sat and begged? Others said, It is he : others said, No, but he is like him. He said, I am *he.* They said therefore unto him, How then were thine eyes opened? He answered, The man that is called Jesus made clay, and anointed mine eyes, and said unto me, Go to Siloam, and wash : so I went away and washed, and I received sight. And they said unto him, Where is he? He said, I know not.

They bring to the Pharisees him that aforetime was blind. Now it was the sabbath on the day when Jesus made the clay, and opened his eyes. Again therefore the Pharisees also asked him how he received his sight. And he said unto them, He put clay upon mine eyes, and I washed, and do see. Some therefore of the Pharisees said, This man is not from God, because he keepeth not the sabbath. But others said, How can a man that is a sinner do such signs? And there was a division among them. They say therefore unto the blind man again, What sayest thou of him, in that he opened thine eyes? And he said, He is a prophet. The Jews therefore did not believe concerning him, that he had been blind, and had received his sight, until they called the parents of him that had received his sight, and asked them, saying, Is this your son, who ye say was born blind? how then doth he now see? His parents answered and said, We[1]

---

1. John 9 : 1-20.

know that this is our son, and that he was born blind : but how he now seeth, we know not; or who opened his eyes, we know not : ask him ; he is of age ; he shall speak for himself. These things said his parents, because they feared the Jews : for the Jews had agreed already, that if any man should confess him *to be* Christ, he should be put out of the synagogue. Therefore said his parents, He is of age ; ask him. So they called a second time the man that was blind, and said unto him, Give glory to God : we know that this man is a sinner. He therefore answered, Whether he be a sinner, I know not : one thing I know, that, whereas I was blind, now I see. They said therefore unto him, What did he to thee ? how opened he thine eyes ? He answered them, I told you even now, and ye did not hear : wherefore would ye hear it again ? would ye also become his disciples ? And they reviled him, and said, Thou art his disciple ; but we are disciples of Moses. We know that God hath spoken unto Moses : but as for this man, we know not whence he is. The man answered and said unto them, Why, herein is the marvel, that ye know not whence he is, and *yet* he opened mine eyes. We know that God heareth not sinners : but if any man be a worshipper of God, and do his will, him he heareth. Since the world began it was never heard that any one opened the eyes of a man born blind. If this man were not from God, he could do nothing. They answered and said unto him, Thou wast altogether born in sins, and dost thou teach us ? And they cast him out.

Jesus heard that they had cast him out ; and finding him, he said, Dost thou believe on the Son of God ? He answered and said, And who is he, Lord, that I may believe on him ? Jesus said unto him, Thou hast both seen him, and he it is that speaketh with thee. And he said, Lord, I believe. And he worshipped him. And Jesus said, For judgement came I into this world, that they which see not may see ; and that they which see may become blind. Those of the Pharisees which were with him heard these things, and said unto him, Are we also blind ? Jesus said unto them, If ye were blind, ye would have no sin : but now ye say, We see : your sin remaineth.[1]

---

1. John 9: 20-41.

§ 67—JESUS THE GOOD SHEPHERD.

Verily, verily, I say unto you, He that entereth not by the door into the fold of the sheep, but climbeth up some other way, the same is a thief and a robber. But he that entereth in by the door is the shepherd of the sheep. To him the porter openeth ; and the sheep hear his voice : and he calleth his own sheep by name, and leadeth them out. When he hath put forth all his own, he goeth before them, and the sheep follow him : for they know his voice. And a stranger will they not follow, but will flee from him : for they know not the voice of strangers. This parable spake Jesus unto them : but they understood not what things they were which he spake unto them.

Jesus therefore said unto them again, Verily, verily, I say unto you, I am the door of the sheep. All that came before me are thieves and robbers : but the sheep did not hear them. I am the door : by me if any man enter in, he shall be saved, and shall go in and go out, and shall find pasture. The thief cometh not, but that he may steal, and kill, and destroy : I came that they may have life, and may have *it* abundantly. I am the good shepherd : the good shepherd layeth down his life for the sheep. He that is a hireling, and not a shepherd, whose own the sheep are not, beholdeth the wolf coming, and leaveth the sheep, and fleeth, and the wolf snatcheth them, and scattereth *them* : *he fleeth* because he is a hireling, and careth not for the sheep. I am the good shepherd ; and I know mine own, and mine own know me, even as the Father knoweth me, and I know the Father ; and I lay down my life for the sheep. And other sheep I have, which are not of this fold : them also I must bring, and they shall hear my voice ; and they shall become one flock, one shepherd. Therefore doth the Father love me, because I lay down my life, that I may take it again. No one taketh it away from me, but I lay it down of myself. I have power to lay it down, and I have power to take it again. This commandment received I from my Father.[1]

---

1. John 10 : 1-18.

There arose a division again among the Jews because of these words. And many of them said, He hath a devil, and is mad ; why hear ye him ? Others said, These are not the sayings of one possessed with a devil. Can a devil open the eyes of the blind?[1]

§ 68—JESUS TEACHES THAT HE IS THE SON OF GOD.

And it was the feast of the dedication at Jerusalem : it was winter ; and Jesus was walking in the temple in Solomon's porch. The Jews therefore came round about him, and said unto him, How long dost thou hold us in suspense ? If thou art the Christ, tell us plainly. Jesus answered them, I told you, and ye believe not : the works that I do in my Father's name, these bear witness of me. But ye believe not, because ye are not of my sheep. My sheep hear my voice, and I know them, and they follow me : and I give unto them eternal life ; and they shall never perish, and no one shall snatch them out of my hand. My Father, which hath given *them* unto me, is greater than all ; and no one is able to snatch *them* out of the Father's hand. I and the Father are one. The Jews took up stones again to stone him. Jesus answered them, Many good works have I shewed you from the Father ; for which of those works do ye stone me ? The Jews answered him, For a good work we stone thee not, but for blasphemy; and because that thou, being a man, makest thyself God. Jesus answered them, Is it not written in your law, I said, Ye are gods ? If he called them gods, unto whom the word of God came (and the scripture cannot be broken), say ye of him, whom the Father sanctified and sent into the world, Thou blasphemest ; because I said, I am *the* Son of God ? If I do not the works of my Father, believe me not. But if I do them, though ye believe not me, believe the works : that ye may know and understand that the Father is in me, and I in the Father. They sought again to take him : and he went forth out of their hand.[2]

---

1. John 10 : 19-21.   2. John 10 : 22-39.

And he went away again beyond Jordan into the place where John was at the first baptizing; and there he abode. And many came unto him; and they said, John indeed did no sign : but all things whatsoever John spake of this man were true. And many believed on him there.[1]

§ 69—THE DEATH OF LAZARUS.

Now a certain man was sick, Lazarus of Bethany, of the village of Mary and her sister Martha. And it was that Mary which anointed the Lord with ointment, and wiped his feet with her hair, whose brother Lazarus was sick. The sisters therefore sent unto him, saying, Lord, behold, he whom thou lovest is sick. But when Jesus heard it, he said, This sickness is not unto death, but for the glory of God, that the Son of God may be glorified thereby. Now Jesus loved Martha, and her sister, and Lazarus. When therefore he heard that he was sick, he abode at that time two days in the place where he was. Then after this he saith to the disciples, Let us go into Judæa again. The disciples say unto him, Rabbi, the Jews were but now seeking to stone thee ; and goest thou thither again? Jesus answered, Are there not twelve hours in the day? If a man walk in the day, he stumbleth not, because he seeth the light of this world. But if a man walk in the night, he stumbleth, because the light is not in him. These things spake he : and after this he saith unto them, Our friend Lazarus is fallen asleep; but I go, that I may awake him out of sleep. The disciples therefore said unto him, Lord, if he is fallen asleep, he will recover. Now Jesus had spoken of his death: but they thought that he spake of taking rest in sleep. Then Jesus therefore said unto them plainly, Lazarus is dead. And I am glad for your sakes that I was not there, to the intent ye may believe ; nevertheless let us go unto him. Thomas therefore, who is called Didymus, said unto his fellow-disciples, Let us also go, that we may die with him.[2]

---

1. John 10 : 40-42.   2. John 11 : 1-16.

§ 70—THE JOURNEY TO BETHANY.

And he went on his way through cities and villages, teaching, and journeying on unto Jerusalem. And one said unto him, Lord, are they few that be saved? And he said unto them, Strive to enter in by the narrow door : for many, I say unto you, shall seek to enter in, and shall not be able. When once the master of the house is risen up, and hath shut to the door, and ye begin to stand without, and to knock at the door, saying, Lord, open to us ; and he shall answer and say to you, I know you not whence ye are ; then shall ye begin to say, We did eat and drink in thy presence, and thou didst teach in our streets ; and he shall say, I tell you, I know not whence ye are ; depart from me, all ye workers of iniquity. There shall be the weeping and gnashing of teeth, when ye shall see Abraham, and Isaac, and Jacob, and all the prophets, in the kingdom of God, and yourselves cast forth without. And they shall come from the east and west, and from the north and south, and shall sit down in the kingdom of God. And behold, there are last which shall be first, and there are first which shall be last.

In that very hour there came certain Pharisees, saying to him, Get thee out, and go hence : for Herod would fain kill thee. And he said unto them, Go and say to that fox, Behold, I cast out devils and perform cures to-day and to-morrow, and the third *day* I am perfected. Howbeit I must go on my way to-day and to-morrow and the *day* following : for it cannot be that a prophet perish out of Jerusalem. O Jerusalem, Jerusalem, which killeth the prophets, and stoneth them that are sent unto her ! how often would I have gathered thy children together, even as a hen *gathereth* her own brood under her wings, and ye would not ! Behold, your house is left unto you *desolate* : and I say unto you, Ye shall not see me, until ye shall say, Blessed *is* he that cometh in the name of the Lord.[1]

---

1. Luke 13 : 22-35.

And it came to pass, when he went into the house of one
of the rulers of the Pharisees on a sabbath to eat bread, that
they were watching him. And behold, there was before him
a certain man which had the dropsy. And Jesus answering
spake unto the lawyers and Pharisees, saying, Is it lawful to
heal on the sabbath, or not? But they held their peace.
And he took him, and healed him, and let him go. And he
said unto them, Which of you shall have an ass or an ox
fallen into a well, and will not straightway draw him up on
a sabbath day? And they could not answer again unto these
things.[1]

§ 71—THE PARABLES OF THE GREAT SUPPER, THE
LOST SHEEP, AND THE LOST PIECE OF SILVER.

And he spake a parable unto those which were bidden,
when he marked how they chose out the chief seats ; saying
unto them, When thou art bidden of any man to a marriage
feast, sit not down in the chief seat ; lest haply a more honourable man than thou be bidden of him, and he that bade
thee and him shall come and say to thee, Give this man
place ; and then thou shalt begin with shame to take the
lowest place. But when thou art bidden, go and sit down
in the lowest place ; that when he that hath bidden thee
cometh, he may say to thee, Friend, go up higher : then
shalt thou have glory in the presence of all that sit at meat
with thee. For every one that exalteth himself shall be
humbled ; and he that humbleth himself shall be exalted.

And he said to him also that had bidden him, When thou
makest a dinner or a supper, call not thy friends, nor thy
brethren, nor thy kinsmen, nor rich neighbours ; lest haply
they also bid thee again, and a recompense be made thee.
But when thou makest a feast, bid the poor, the maimed, the
lame, the blind : and thou shalt be blessed ; because they
have not *wherewith* to recompense thee : for thou shalt be
recompensed in the resurrection of the just.[2]

---

1. Luke 14 : 1-6.   2. Luke 14 : 7-14.

And when one of them that sat at meat with him heard these things, he said unto him, Blessed is he that shall eat bread in the kingdom of God. But he said unto him, A certain man made a great supper ; and he bade many : and he sent forth his servant at supper time to say to them that were bidden, Come ; for *all* things are now ready. And they all with one *consent* began to make excuse. The first said unto him, I have bought a field, and I must needs go out and see it : I pray thee have me excused. And another said, I have bought five yoke of oxen, and I go to prove them : I pray thee have me excused. And another said, I have married a wife, and therefore I cannot come. And the servant came, and told his lord these things. Then the master of the house being angry said to his servant, Go out quickly into the streets and lanes of the city, and bring in hither the poor and maimed and blind and lame. And the servant said, Lord, what thou didst command is done, and yet there is room. And the lord said unto the servant, Go out into the highways and hedges, and constrain *them* to come in, that my house may be filled. For I say unto you, that none of those men which were bidden shall taste of my supper.

Now there went with him great multitudes : and he turned, and said unto them, If any man cometh unto me, and hateth not his own father, and mother, and wife, and children, and brethren, and sisters, yea, and his own life also, he cannot be my disciple. Whosoever doth not bear his own cross, and come after me, cannot be my disciple. For which of you, desiring to build a tower, doth not first sit down and count the cost, whether he have *wherewith* to complete it ? Lest haply, when he hath laid a foundation, and is not able to finish, all that behold begin to mock him, saying, This man began to build, and was not able to finish. Or what king, as he goeth to encounter another king in war, will not sit down first and take counsel whether he is able with ten thousand to meet him that cometh against him with twenty thousand ? Or else, while the other is yet a great way off,[1]

---

1. Luke 14 : 15-32.

he sendeth an ambassage, and asketh conditions of peace. So therefore whosoever he be of you that renounceth not all that he hath, he cannot be my disciple. Salt therefore is good : but if even the salt have lost its savour, wherewith shall it be seasoned ? It is fit neither for the land nor for the dunghill : *men* cast it out. He that hath ears to hear, let him hear.[1]

Now all the publicans and sinners were drawing near unto him for to hear him. And both the Pharisees and the scribes murmured, saying, This man receiveth sinners, and eateth with them.

And he spake unto them this parable, saying, What man of you, having a hundred sheep, and having lost one of them, doth not leave the ninety and nine in the wilderness, and go after that which is lost, until he find it ? And when he hath found it, he layeth it on his shoulders, rejoicing. And when he cometh home, he calleth together his friends and his neighbours, saying unto them, Rejoice with me, for I have found my sheep which was lost. I say unto you, that even so there shall be joy in heaven over one sinner that repenteth, *more* than over ninety and nine righteous persons, which need no repentance.

Or what woman having ten pieces of silver, if she lose one piece, doth not light a lamp, and sweep the house, and seek diligently until she find it ? And when she hath found it, she calleth together her friends and neighbours, saying, Rejoice with me, for I have found the piece which I had lost. Even so, I say unto you, there is joy in the presence of the angels of God over one sinner that repenteth.[2]

§ 72—THE PARABLE OF THE PRODIGAL SON.

And he said, A certain man had two sons : and the younger of them said to his father, Father, give me the portion of *thy* substance that falleth to me. And he divided unto them his living. And not many days after the younger son gathered all together, and took his journey into a far country ; and there he wasted his substance with riotous

1. Luke 14 : 32-35.   2. Luke 15 : 1-10.

living. And when he had spent all, there arose a mighty famine in that country ; and he began to be in want. And he went and joined himself to one of the citizens of that country; and he sent him into his fields to feed swine. And he would fain have been filled with the husks that the swine did eat : and no man gave unto him. But when he came to himself he said, How many hired servants of my father's have bread enough and to spare, and I perish here with hunger ! I will arise and go to my father, and will say unto him, Father, I have sinned against heaven, and in thy sight : I am no more worthy to be called thy son : make me as one of thy hired servants. And he arose, and came to his father. But while he was yet afar off, his father saw him, and was moved with compassion, and ran, and fell on his neck, and kissed him. And the son said unto him, Father, I have sinned against heaven, and in thy sight : I am no more worthy to be called thy son. But the father said to his servants, Bring forth quickly the best robe, and put it on him ; and put a ring on his hand, and shoes on his feet : and bring the fatted calf, *and* kill it, and let us eat, and make merry: for this my son was dead, and is alive again ; he was lost, and is found. And they began to be merry. Now his elder son was in the field : and as he came and drew nigh to the house, he heard music and dancing. And he called to him one of the servants, and inquired what these things might be. And he said unto him, Thy brother is come ; and thy father hath killed the fatted calf, because he hath received him safe and sound. But he was angry, and would not go in : and his father came out, and intreated him. But he answered and said to his father, Lo, these many years do I serve thee, and I never transgressed a commandment of thine : and *yet* thou never gavest me a kid, that I might make merry with my friends : but when this thy son came, which hath devoured thy living with harlots, thou killedst for him the fatted calf. And he said unto him, Son, thou art ever with me, and all that is mine is thine. But it was meet to make merry and be glad : for this thy brother was dead, and is alive *again* ; and *was* lost, and is found.[1]

---

1. Luke 15 : 11-32.

§ 73—THE PARABLES OF THE UNJUST STEWARD AND OF DIVES AND LAZARUS.

And he said also unto the disciples, There was a certain rich man, which had a steward; and the same was accused unto him that he was wasting his goods. And he called him, and said unto him, What is this that I hear of thee? render the account of thy stewardship; for thou canst be no longer steward. And the steward said within himself, What shall I do, seeing that my lord taketh away the stewardship from me? I have not strength to dig; to beg I am ashamed. I am resolved what to do, that, when I am put out of the stewardship, they may receive me into their houses. And calling to him each one of his lord's debtors, he said to the first, How much owest thou unto my lord? And he said, A hundred measures of oil. And he said unto him, Take thy bond, and sit down quickly and write fifty. Then said he to another, And how much owest thou? And he said, A hundred measures of wheat. He saith unto him, Take thy bond, and write fourscore. And his lord commended the unrighteous steward because he had done wisely: for the sons of this world are for their own generation wiser than the sons of the light. And I say unto you, Make to yourselves friends by means of the mammon of unrighteousness; that, when it shall fail, they may receive you into the eternal tabernacles. He that is faithful in a very little is faithful also in much: and he that is unrighteous in a very little is unrighteous also in much. If therefore ye have not been faithful in the unrighteous mammon, who will commit to your trust the true *riches?* And if ye have not been faithful in that which is another's, who will give you that which is your own? No servant can serve two masters: for either he will hate the one, and love the other; or else he will hold to one, and despise the other. Ye cannot serve God and mammon.[1]

---

1. Luke 16 : 1-13.

Now there was a certain rich man, and he was clothed in purple and fine linen, faring sumptuously every day: and a certain beggar named Lazarus was laid at his gate, full of sores, and desiring to be fed with the *crumbs* that fell from the rich man's table; yea, even the dogs came and licked his sores. And it came to pass, that the beggar died, and that he was carried away by the angels into Abraham's bosom: and the rich man also died, and was buried. And in Hades he lifted up his eyes, being in torments, and seeth Abraham afar off, and Lazarus in his bosom. And he cried and said, Father Abraham, have mercy on me, and send Lazarus, that he may dip the tip of his finger in water, and cool my tongue; for I am in anguish in this flame. But Abraham said, Son, remember that thou in thy lifetime receivedst thy good things, and Lazarus in like manner evil things: but now here he is comforted, and thou art in anguish. And beside all this, between us and you there is a great gulf fixed, that they which would pass from hence to you may not be able, and that none may cross over from thence to us. And he said, I pray thee therefore, father, that thou wouldest send him to my father's house; for I have five brethren; that he may testify unto them, lest they also come into this place of torment. But Abraham saith, They have Moses and the prophets; let them hear them. And he said, Nay, father Abraham: but if one go to them from the dead, they will repent. And he said unto him, If they hear not Moses and the prophets, neither will they be persuaded, if one rise from the dead.[1]

§ 74—THE RAISING OF LAZARUS.

So when Jesus came [to Bethany] he found that he had been in the tomb four days already. Now Bethany was nigh unto Jerusalem, about fifteen furlongs off; and many of the Jews had come to Martha and Mary, to console them concerning their brother. Martha therefore, when she heard that Jesus was coming, went and met him: but Mary still

---

1. Luke 16 : 19-31.

sat in the house. Martha therefore said unto Jesus, Lord,
if thou hadst been here, my brother had not died. And
even now I know that, whatsoever thou shalt ask of God,
God will give thee. Jesus saith unto her. Thy brother
shall rise again. Martha saith unto him, I know that he
shall rise again in the resurrection at the last day. Jesus
said unto her, I am the resurrection and the life : he that
believeth on me, though he die, yet shall he live : and whosoever liveth and believeth on me shall never die. Believest
thou this ? She saith unto him, Yea, Lord: I have believed
that thou art the Christ, the Son of God, *even* he that cometh
into the world. And when she had said this, she went away,
and called Mary her sister secretly, saying, The Master is here,
and calleth thee. And she, when she heard it, arose quickly,
and went unto him. (Now Jesus was not yet come into the
village, but was still in the place where Martha met him.)
The Jews then which were with her in the house, and were
comforting her, when they saw Mary, that she rose up quickly
and went out, followed her, supposing that she was going
unto the tomb to weep there. Mary therefore, when she
came where Jesus was, and saw him, fell down at his feet,
saying unto him, Lord, if thou hadst been here, my brother
had not died. When Jesus therefore saw her weeping, and
the Jews *also* weeping which came with her, he groaned in
the spirit, and was troubled, and said, Where have ye laid
him ? They say unto him, Lord, come and see. Jesus wept.
The Jews therefore said, Behold how he loved him ! But
some of them said, Could not this man, which opened the
eyes of him that was blind, have caused that this man also
should not die ? Jesus therefore again groaning in himself
cometh to the tomb. Now it was a cave, and a stone lay
against it. Jesus saith, Take ye away the stone. Martha,
the sister of him that was dead, saith unto him, Lord, by
this time he stinketh : for he hath been *dead* four days.
Jesus saith unto her, Said I not unto thee, that, if thou believedst, thou shouldest see the glory of God ? So they took
away the stone. And Jesus lifted up his eyes, and said,[1]

1. John 11 : 17-41.

Father, I thank thee that thou heardest me.   And I knew
that thou hearest me always : but because of the multitude
which standeth around I said it, that they may believe that
thou didst send me.   And when he had thus spoken, he cried
with a loud voice, Lazarus, come forth.   He that was dead
came forth, bound hand and foot with grave-clothes ; and his
face was bound about with a napkin.   Jesus saith unto them,
Loose him, and let him go.

Many therefore of the Jews, which came to Mary and beheld that which he did, believed on him.   But some of them
went away to the Pharisees, and told them the things which
Jesus had done.

The chief priests therefore and the Pharisees gathered a
council, and said, What do we ? for this man doeth many
signs.   If we let him thus alone, all men will believe on
him : and the Romans will come and take away both our
place and our nation.   But a certain one of them, Caiaphas,
being high priest that year, said unto them, Ye know nothing at all, nor do ye take account that it is expedient for you
that one man should die for the people, and that the whole
nation perish not.   Now this he said not of himself : but
being high priest that year, he prophesied that Jesus should
die for the nation ; and not for the nation only, but that he
might also gather together into one the children of God that
are scattered abroad.   So from that day forth they took
counsel that they might put him to death.

Jesus therefore walked no more openly among the Jews,
but departed thence into the country near to the wilderness,
into a city called Ephraim ; and there he tarried with the
disciples.[1]

§75—JESUS AGAIN VISITS JERUSALEM.

And it came to pass when Jesus had finished these words,
he departed from Galilee, and came into the borders of
Judæa beyond Jordan; and great[2] multitudes came together
unto him again ; and as he was wont, he taught them
again.[3]

---

1. John 11 : 41-54.   2. Matt. 19 : 1, 2.   3. Mark 10 : 1.

And it came to pass, when the days were well-nigh come that he should be received up, he stedfastly set his face to go to Jerusalem, and sent messengers before his face : and they went, and entered into a village of the Samaritans, to make ready for him.   And they did not receive him, because his face was *as though he were* going to Jerusalem.   And when his disciples James and John saw *this*, they said, Lord, wilt thou that we bid fire to come down from heaven, and consume them ?   But he turned, and rebuked them.   And they went to another village.

And as they went in the way, a certain man said unto him, I will follow thee whithersoever thou goest.   And Jesus said unto him, The foxes have holes, and the birds of the heaven *have* nests ; but the Son of man hath not where to lay his head.   And he said unto another, Follow me.   But he said, Lord, suffer me first to go and bury my father.   But he said unto him, Leave the dead to bury their own dead ; but go thou and publish abroad the kingdom of God.   And another also said, I will follow thee, Lord ; but first suffer me to bid farewell to them that are at my house. But Jesus said unto him, No man, having put his hand to the plough, and looking back, is fit for the kingdom of God.[1]

§ 76—THE SENDING FORTH AND RETURN OF THE SEVENTY.

Now after these things the Lord appointed seventy others, and sent them two and two before his face into every city and place, whither he himself was about to come.   And he said unto them, The harvest is plenteous, but the labourers are few : pray ye therefore the Lord of the harvest, that he send forth labourers into his harvest.   Go your ways : behold, I send you forth as lambs in the midst of wolves. Carry no purse, no wallet, no shoes : and salute no man on the way.   And into whatsoever house ye shall enter, first say, Peace *be* to this house.   And if a son of peace be there,

---

1. Luke 9 : 51-62.

your peace shall rest upon him : but if not, it shall turn to you again. And in that same house remain, eating and drinking such things as they give : for the labourer is worthy of his hire. Go not from house to house. And into whatsoever city ye enter, and they receive you, eat such things as are set before you : and heal the sick that are therein, and say unto them, The kingdom of God is come nigh unto you. But into whatsoever city ye shall enter, and they receive you not, go out into the streets thereof and say, Even the dust from your city, that cleaveth to our feet, we do wipe off against you : howbeit know this, that the kingdom of God is come nigh. I say unto you, It shall be more tolerable in that day for Sodom, than for that city.[1]

Then began he to upbraid the cities wherein most of his mighty works were done, because they repented not. Woe unto thee, Chorazin ! woe unto thee, Bethsaida ! for if the mighty works had been done in Tyre and Sidon which were done in you, they would have repented long ago in sackcloth and ashes. Howbeit I say unto you, it shall be more tolerable for Tyre and Sidon in the day of judgement than for you. And thou, Capernaum, shalt thou be exalted unto heaven ? thou shalt go down unto Hades : for if the mighty works had been done in Sodom which were done in thee, it would have remained until this day. Howbeit I say unto you, that it shall be more tolerable for the land of Sodom in the day of judgement, than for thee.[2] He that heareth you heareth me ; and he that rejecteth you rejecteth me ; and he that rejecteth me rejecteth him that sent me.

And the seventy returned with joy, saying, Lord, even the devils are subject unto us in thy name. And he said unto them, I beheld Satan fallen as lightning from heaven. Behold, I have given you authority to tread upon serpents and scorpions, and over all the power of the enemy : and nothing shall in any wise hurt you. Howbeit in this rejoice not, that the spirits are subject unto you ; but rejoice that your names are written in heaven.[3]

---

1. Luke 10 : 1-12.   2. Matt. 11 : 20-24.   3. Luke 10 : 16-20.

In that same hour he rejoiced in the Holy Spirit, and said, I thank thee, O Father, Lord of heaven and earth, that thou didst hide these things from the wise and understanding, and didst reveal them unto babes : yea, Father ; for so it was well-pleasing in thy sight. All things have been delivered unto me of my Father : and no one knoweth who the Son is, save the Father ; and who the Father is, save the Son, and he to whomsoever the Son willeth to reveal *him*.[1] Come unto me, all ye that labour and are heavy laden, and I will give you rest. Take my yoke upon you, and learn of me ; for I am meek and lowly in heart : and ye shall find rest unto your souls. For my yoke is easy, and my burden is light.[2]

And turning to the disciples, he said privately, Blessed *are* the eyes which see the things that ye see : for I say unto you, that many prophets and kings desired to see the things which ye see, and saw them not ; and to hear the things which ye hear, and heard them not.[3]

§ 77—THE PARABLE OF THE GOOD SAMARITAN.

And behold, a certain lawyer stood up and tempted him, saying, Master, what shall I do to inherit eternal life ? And he said unto him, What is written in the law ? how readest thou ? And he answering said, Thou shalt love the Lord thy God with all thy heart, and with all thy soul, and with all thy strength, and with all thy mind ; and thy neighbour as thyself. And he said unto him, Thou hast answered right : this do, and thou shalt live. But he, desiring to justify himself, said unto Jesus, And who is my neighbour ? Jesus made answer and said, A certain man was going down from Jerusalem to Jericho ; and he fell among robbers, which both stripped him and beat him, and departed, leaving him half dead. And by chance a certain priest was going down that way : and when he saw him, he passed by on the other side. And in like manner a Levite also, when he came to the place, and saw him, passed by on

---

1. Luke 10 : 21, 22.   2. Matt. 11 : 28-30.   3. Luke 10 : 23, 24.

the other side. But a certain Samaritan, as he journeyed, came where he was: and when he saw him, he was moved with compassion, and came to him, and bound up his wounds, pouring on *them* oil and wine; and he set him on his own beast, and brought him to an inn, and took care of him. And on the morrow he took out two pence, and gave them to the host, and said, Take care of him; and whatsoever thou spendest more, I, when I come back again, will repay thee. Which of these three, thinkest thou, proved neighbour unto him that fell among the robbers? And he said, He that shewed mercy on him. And Jesus said unto him, Go, and do thou likewise.[1]

§ 78—MARY CHOOSES THE " GOOD PART."

Now as they went on their way, he entered into a certain village: and a certain woman named Martha received him into her house. And she had a sister called Mary, which also sat at the Lord's feet, and heard his word. But Martha was cumbered about much serving; and she came up to him, and said, Lord, dost thou not care that my sister did leave me to serve alone? bid her therefore that she help me. But the Lord answered and said unto her, Martha, Martha, thou art anxious and troubled about many things: but one thing is needful: for Mary hath chosen the good part, which shall not be taken away from her.[2]

§ 79—JESUS TEACHES PERSEVERANCE IN PRAYER.

And it came to pass, as he was praying in a certain place, that when he ceased, one of his disciples said unto him, Lord, teach us to pray, even as John also taught his disciples. And he said unto them, When ye pray, say, Father, Hallowed be thy name. Thy kingdom come. Give us day by day our daily bread. And forgive us our sins; for we ourselves also forgive every one that is indebted to us. And bring us not into temptation.

---

1. Luke 10 : 25-37.   2. Luke 10 : 38-42.

And he said unto them, Which of you shall have a friend, and shall go unto him at midnight, and say to him, Friend, lend me three loaves; for a friend of mine is come to me from a journey, and I have nothing to set before him; and he from within shall answer and say, Trouble me not: the door is now shut, and my children are with me in bed; I cannot rise and give thee? I say unto you, Though he will not rise and give him, because he is his friend, yet because of his importunity he will arise and give him as many as he needeth. And I say unto you, Ask, and it shall be given you; seek, and ye shall find; knock, and it shall be opened unto you. For every one that asketh receiveth; and he that seeketh findeth; and to him that knocketh it shall be opened. And of which of you that is a father shall his son ask a loaf, and he give him a stone? or a fish, and he for a fish give him a serpent? Or *if* he shall ask an egg, will he give him a scorpion? If ye then, being evil, know how to give good gifts unto your children, how much more shall *your* heavenly Father give the Holy Spirit to them that ask him?[1]

§ 80—JESUS TEACHES FORGIVENESS AND FAITH.

And he said unto his disciples, It is impossible but that occasions of stumbling should come: but woe unto him, through whom they come! It were well for him if a millstone were hanged about his neck, and he were thrown into the sea, rather than that he should cause one of these little ones to stumble. Take heed to yourselves: if thy brother sin, rebuke him; and if he repent, forgive him. And if he sin against thee seven times in the day, and seven times turn again to thee, saying, I repent; thou shalt forgive him.

And the apostles said unto the Lord, Increase our faith. And the Lord said, If ye have faith as a grain of mustard seed, ye would say unto this sycamine tree, Be thou rooted up, and be thou planted in the sea; and it would have obeyed you. But who is there of you, having a servant

---

1. Luke 11 : 1-13.

plowing or keeping sheep, that will say unto him, when he
is come in from the field, Come straightway and sit down to
meat; and will not rather say unto him, Make ready wherewith I may sup, and gird thyself, and serve me, till I have
eaten and drunken ; and afterward thou shalt eat and drink ?
Doth he thank the servant because he did the things that
were commanded ?   Even so ye also, when ye shall have
done all the things that are commanded you, say, We are
unprofitable servants; we have done that which it was our
duty to do.[1]

§ 81—JESUS CLEANSES TEN LEPERS.

And it came to pass, as they were on the way to Jerusalem,
that he was passing through the midst of Samaria and Galilee.   And as he entered into a certain village, there met him
ten men that were lepers, which stood afar off : and they
lifted up their voices, saying, Jesus, Master, have mercy on
us.   And when he saw them, he said unto them, Go and
shew yourselves unto the priests.   And it came to pass, as
they went, they were cleansed.   And one of them, when he
saw that he was healed, turned back, with a loud voice glorifying God : and he fell upon his face at his feet, giving him
thanks: and he was a Samaritan.   And Jesus answering
said, Were not the ten cleansed ? but where are the nine ?
Were there none found that returned to give glory to God,
save this stranger ?   And he saith unto him, Arise, and go
thy way, thy faith hath made thee whole.[2]

§ 82—JESUS FORETELLS THE SUDDENNESS OF
JUDGEMENT.

And being asked by the Pharisees, when the kingdom of
God cometh, he answered them and said, The kingdom of
God cometh not with observation : neither shall they say,
Lo, here ! or, There! for lo, the kingdom of God is within
you.

---

1. Luke 17 : 1-10.   2. Luke 17 : 11-19.

And he said unto the disciples, The days will come, when
ye shall desire to see one of the days of the Son of man, and
ye shall not see it   And they shall say to you, Lo, there ! Lo,
here ! go not away, nor follow after *them* : for as the lightning,
when it lighteneth out of the one part under the heaven,
shineth unto the other part under heaven ; so shall the Son
of man be in his day.   But first must he suffer many things
and be rejected of this generation.   And as it came to pass
in the days of Noah, even so shall it be also in the days of
the Son of man.   They ate, they drank, they married, they
were given in marriage, until the day that Noah entered into
the ark, and the flood came, and destroyed them all.   Likewise even as it came to pass in the days of Lot ; they ate,
they drank, they bought, they sold, they planted, they
builded ; but in the day that Lot went out from Sodom it
rained fire and brimstone from heaven, and destroyed them
all : after the same manner shall it be in the day that the
Son of man is revealed.   In that day, he which shall be on
the housetop, and his goods in the house, let him not go
down to take them away : and let him that is in the field
likewise not return back   Remember Lot's wife.   Whosoever
shall seek to gain his life shall lose it : but whosoever shall
lose *his life* shall preserve it.   I say unto you, In that night
there shall be two men on one bed ; the one shall be taken,
and the other shall be left.   There shall be two women
grinding together ; the one shall be taken, and the other
shall be left.   And they answering say unto him, Where,
Lord ?   And he said unto them, Where the body *is*, thither
will the eagles also be gathered together.[1]

§ 83—THE PARABLES OF THE UNRIGHTEOUS JUDGE
AND OF THE PHARISEE AND THE PUBLICAN.

And he spake a parable unto them to the end that they
ought always to pray, and not to faint ; saying, There was
in a city a judge, which feared not God, and regarded not

---

1. Luke 17 : 20-37.

man: and there was a widow in that city; and she came oft unto him, saying, Avenge me of mine adversary. And he would not for a while: but afterward he said within himself, Though I fear not God, nor regard man; yet because this widow troubleth me, I will avenge her, lest she wear me out by her continual coming. And the Lord said, Hear what the unrighteous judge saith. And shall not God avenge his elect, which cry to him day and night, and he is longsuffering over them? I say unto you, that he will avenge them speedily. Howbeit when the Son of man cometh, shall he find faith on the earth?

And he spake also this parable unto certain which trusted in themselves that they were righteous, and set all others at nought: Two men went up into the temple to pray; the one a Pharisee, and the other a publican. The Pharisee stood and prayed thus with himself, God, I thank thee, that I am not as the rest of men, extortioners, unjust, adulterers, or even as this publican. I fast twice in the week; I give tithes of all that I get. But the publican, standing afar off, would not lift up so much as his eyes unto heaven, but smote his breast, saying, God, be merciful to me a sinner. I say unto you, This man went down to his house justified rather than the other: for every man that exalteth himself shall be humbled; but he that humbleth himself shall be exalted.[1]

§ 84—JESUS DISCOURSES ON MARRIAGE AND DIVORCE.

And there came unto him Pharisees, tempting him, and saying, Is it lawful *for a man* to put away his wife for every cause?[2] And he answered and said unto them, What did Moses command you? And they said, Moses suffered to write a bill of divorcement, and to put her away. But Jesus said unto them, For your hardness of heart he wrote you this commandment. But from the beginning of the creation,

---

1. Luke 18: 1-14.　　2. Matt. 19: 3.

Male and female made he them. For this cause shall a
man leave his father and mother, and shall cleave to his
wife; and the twain shall become one flesh: so that they are
no more twain, but one flesh. What therefore God hath
joined together, let no man put asunder. And in the house
the disciples asked him again of this matter,[1] [and] they
say unto him, Why then did Moses command to give a bill
of divorcement, and to put *her* away? He saith unto them,
Moses for your hardness of heart suffered you to put away
your wives: but from the beginning it hath not been so.
And I say unto you, Whosoever shall put away his wife,
except for fornication, and shall marry another, committeth
adultery:[2] and if she herself shall put away her husband,
and marry another, she committeth adultery.[3] And he that
marrieth her when she is put away committeth adultery.
The disciples say unto him, If the case of the man is so
with his wife, it is not expedient to marry. But he said
unto them, All men cannot receive this saying, but they to
whom it is given. For there are eunuchs, which were so
born from their mother's womb: and there are eunuchs,
which were made eunuchs by men: and there are eunuchs,
which made themselves eunuchs for the kingdom of heaven's
sake. He that is able to receive it, let him receive it.[4]

§ 85—JESUS BLESSES LITTLE CHILDREN.

And they brought unto him little children, that he should[5]
lay his hands on them and pray: and the disciples rebuked
them.[6] But when Jesus saw it, he was moved with indignation.[7] But Jesus called them unto him,[8] and said unto
them, Suffer the little children to come unto me; forbid
them not: for of such is the kingdom of God. Verily I say
unto you, Whosoever shall not receive the kingdom of God
as a little child, he shall in no wise enter therein. And he
took them in his arms, and blessed them, laying his hands
upon them,[9] and departed thence.[10]

---

1. Mark 10 : 3-10.	5. Mark 10 : 13.	8. Luke 18 : 16.
2. Matt. 19 : 7-9.	6. Matt. 19 : 13.	9. Mark 10 : 14-16.
3. Mark 10 : 12.	7. Mark 10 : 14.	10. Matt. 19 : 15.
4. Matt. 19 : 9-12.		

§ 86—THE RICH YOUNG RULER.

And as he was going forth into the way, there ran to him [1] a certain ruler,[2] and kneeled to him, and asked him, Good Master, what shall I do that I may inherit eternal life? And Jesus said unto him, Why callest thou me good? none is good save one, *even* God.[3]

But if thou wouldest enter into life, keep the commandments. He saith unto him, Which? And Jesus said, Thou shalt not kill, Thou shalt not commit adultery, Thou shalt not steal, Thou shalt not bear false witness, Honour thy father and thy mother: and, Thou shalt love thy neighbour as thyself. The young man saith unto him, All these things have I observed [4] from my youth up:[5] what lack I yet?[6] And Jesus looking upon him loved him, and said unto him, One thing thou lackest[7] yet. [8] If thou wouldest be perfect,[9] go, sell whatsoever thou hast, and give to the poor, and thou shalt have treasure in heaven: and come, follow me. But his countenance fell at the saying, and he went away sorrowful: for he was one that had great possessions.

And Jesus looked round about, and saith unto his disciples, How hardly shall they that have riches enter into the kingdom of God! And the disciples were amazed at his words. But Jesus answereth again, and saith unto them, Children, how hard is it for them that trust in riches to enter into the kingdom of God! It is easier for a camel to go through a needle's eye, than for a rich man to enter into the kingdom of God.[10]

And when the disciples heard it, they were astonished exceedingly, saying, Who then can be saved? And Jesus looking upon *them* said to them, With men this is impossible;[11] but not with God: for all things are possible with God.[12] Then answered Peter and said unto him, Lo, we have left all, and followed thee; what then shall we have? And Jesus said

---

1. Mark 10: 17.	5. Luke 18: 21.	9. Matt. 19: 21.
2. Luke 18: 18.	6. Matt. 19: 20.	10. Mark 10: 21-25.
3. Mark 10: 17, 18.	7. Mark 10: 21.	11. Matt. 19: 25, 26.
4. Matt. 19: 17-20.	8. Luke 18: 22.	12. Mark 10: 27.

unto them, Verily I say unto you, that ye which have followed me, in the regeneration when the Son of man shall sit on the throne of his glory, ye also shall sit upon twelve thrones, judging the twelve tribes of Israel.[1] There is no man that hath left house, or brethren, or sisters, or mother, or father, or children, or lands, for my sake, and for the gospel's sake, but he shall receive a hundredfold now in this time, houses, and brethren, and sisters, and mothers, and children, and lands, with persecutions ; and in the world to come eternal life. But many *that are* first shall be last; and the last first.[2]

§ 87—THE PARABLE OF THE LABOURERS IN THE VINEYARD.

For the kingdom of heaven is like unto a man that is a householder, which went out early in the morning to hire labourers into his vineyard. And when he had agreed with the labourers for a penny a day, he sent them into his vineyard. And he went out about the third hour, and saw others standing in the marketplace idle ; and to them he said, Go ye also into the vineyard, and whatsoever is right I will give you. And they went their way. Again he went out about the sixth and the ninth hour, and did likewise. And about the eleventh *hour* he went out, and found others standing ; and he saith unto them, Why stand ye here all the day idle ? They say unto him, Because no man hath hired us. He saith unto them, Go ye also into the vineyard. And when even was come, the lord of the vineyard saith unto his steward, Call the labourers, and pay them their hire, beginning from the last unto the first. And when they came that *were hired* about the eleventh hour, they received every man a penny. And when the first came, they supposed that they would receive more ; and they likewise received every man a penny. And when they received it, they murmured against the householder, saying, These last have spent *but* one hour, and thou hast

---

1. Matt. 19 : 27, 28.   2. Mark 10 : 29-31.

made them equal unto us, which have borne the burden
of the day and the scorching heat. But he answered
and said to one of them, Friend, I do thee no wrong:
didst not thou agree with me for a penny? Take up that
which is thine, and go thy way; it is my will to give unto
this last, even as unto thee. Is it not lawful for me to do
what I will with mine own? or is thine eye evil, because I
am good? So the last shall be first, and the first last.[1]

§88—JESUS FORETELLS HIS DEATH AND RESURRECTION.

And they were in the way, going up to Jerusalem; and
Jesus was going before them: and they were amazed; and
they that followed were afraid. And he took again the
twelve[2] disciples apart,[3] and began to tell them the things
that were to happen unto him, *saying*, Behold, we go up to
Jerusalem;[4] and all the things that are written by the
prophets shall be accomplished unto the Son of man.[5] [And]
he the Son of man shall be delivered unto the chief priests
and the scribes; and they shall condemn him to death,[6] [and]
he shall be delivered up unto the Gentiles, and shall be
mocked, and shamefully entreated, and spit upon: and they
shall scourge and kill him: and the third day he shall rise
again. And they understood none of these things; and this
saying was hid from them, and they perceived not the things
that were said.[7]

Then came to him the mother of the sons of Zebedee with
her sons, worshipping *him*, and asking a certain thing of
him,[8] saying, Master, we would that thou shouldest do for
us whatsoever we shall ask of thee. And he said unto them,
What would ye that I should do for you? And they said
unto him, Grant unto us that we may sit, one on thy right
hand, and one on *thy* left hand, in thy glory. But Jesus
said unto them, Ye know not what ye ask. Are ye able to

---

1. Matt. 20 : 1-16.
2. Mark 10 : 32.
3. Matt. 20 : 17.
4. Mark 10 : 32, 33.
5. Luke 18 : 31.
6. Mark 10 : 33.
7. Luke 18 : 32-34.
8. Matt. 20 : 20.

drink the cup that I drink? or to be baptized with the baptism that I am baptized with? And they said unto him, We are able. And Jesus said unto them, The cup that I drink ye shall drink; and with the baptism that I am baptized withal shall ye be baptized: but to sit on my right hand or on *my* left hand is not mine to give: but *it is for them* for whom it hath been prepared. And when the ten heard it, they began to be moved with indignation concerning James and John. And Jesus called them to him and saith unto them, Ye know that they which are accounted to rule over the Gentiles lord it over them; and their great ones exercise authority over them. But it is not so among you: but whosoever would become great among you, shall be your minister: and whosoever would be first among you, shall be servant of all. For verily the Son of man came not to be ministered unto, but to minister, and to give his life a ransom for many.[1]

§ 89—JESUS GIVES SIGHT TO BLIND BARTIMÆUS AND VISITS ZACCHÆUS.

And they come to Jericho: and as he went out from Jericho, with his disciples and a great multitude, the son of Timæus, Bartimæus, a blind beggar, was sitting by the way side[2] begging: and hearing a multitude going by, he inquired what this meant. And they told him, that Jesus of Nazareth passeth by. And he cried, saying, Jesus, thou son of David, have mercy on me. And they that went before rebuked him, that he should hold his peace: but he cried out the more a great deal, Thou son of David, have mercy on me. And Jesus stood, and commanded him to be brought unto him.[3] And they call the blind man, saying unto him, Be of good cheer: rise, he calleth thee. And he, casting away his garment, sprang up, and came to Jesus.[4] And when he was come near, he asked him, What wilt thou that I should do unto thee? And he said,

---

1. Mark 10: 35-45. 3. Luke 18: 36-40. 4. Mark 10: 49, 50.
2. Mark 10: 46.

Lord, that I may receive my sight. And Jesus said unto him, Receive thy sight : thy faith hath made thee whole. And immediately he received his sight, and followed him, glorifying God ; and all the people, when they saw it, gave praise unto God.[1]

And he entered and was passing through Jericho. And behold, a man called by name Zacchæus ; and he was a chief publican, and he was rich. And he sought to see Jesus who he was ; and could not for the crowd, because he was little of stature. And he ran on before, and climbed up into a sycomore tree to see him : for he was to pass that way. And when Jesus came to the place, he looked up, and said unto him, Zacchæus, make haste, and come down ; for to-day I must abide at thy house. And he made haste, and came down, and received him joyfully. And when they saw it, they all murmured, saying, He is gone in to lodge with a man that is a sinner. And Zacchæus stood, and said unto the Lord, Behold, Lord, the half of my goods I give to the poor ; and if I have wrongfully exacted aught of any man, I restore fourfold. And Jesus said unto him, To-day is salvation come to this house, forasmuch as he also is a son of Abraham. For the Son of man came to seek and to save that which was lost.[2]

§90—THE PARABLE OF THE TEN POUNDS.

And as they heard these things, he added and spake a parable, because he was nigh to Jerusalem, and *because* they supposed that the kingdom of God was immediately to appear. He said therefore, a certain nobleman went into a far country, to receive for himself a kingdom, and to return. And he called ten servants of his, and gave them ten pounds, and said unto them, Trade ye *herewith* till I come. But his citizens hated him, and sent an ambassage after him, saying, We will not that this man reign over us. And it came to pass, when he was come back again, having received the kingdom, that he commanded these servants, unto whom he had given the money, to be

---

1. Luke 18 : 40-43.   2. Luke 19 : 1-10.

called to him, that he might know what they had gained by trading. And the first came before him, saying, Lord, thy pound hath made ten pounds more. And he said unto him, Well done, thou good servant : because thou wast found faithful in a very little, have thou authority over ten cities. And the second came, saying, Thy pound, Lord, hath made five pounds. And he said unto him also, Be thou also over five cities. And another came, saying, Lord, behold, *here is* thy pound, which I kept laid up in a napkin : for I feared thee, because thou art an austere man : thou takest up that thou layedst not down, and reapest that thou didst not sow. He saith unto him, Out of thine own mouth will I judge thee, thou wicked servant. Thou knewest that I am an austere man, taking up that I laid not down, and reaping that I did not sow ; then wherefore gavest thou not my money into the bank, and I at my coming should have required it with interest ? And he said unto them that stood by, Take away from him the pound, and give it unto him that hath the ten pounds. And they said unto him, Lord, he hath ten pounds. I say unto you, that unto every one that hath shall be given ; but from him that hath not, even that which he hath shall be taken away from him. Howbeit these mine enemies, which would not that I should reign over them, bring hither, and slay them before me.[1]

§ 91—THE CHIEF PRIESTS CONSPIRE TO KILL JESUS.

MARY ANOINTS HIM FOR HIS BURIAL.

Now the passover of the Jews was at hand : and many went up to Jerusalem out of the country before the passover, to purify themselves. They sought therefore for Jesus, and spake one with another, as they stood in the temple, What think ye ? That he will not come to the feast ? Now the chief priests and the Pharisees had given commandment, that, if any man knew where he was, he should shew it, that they might take him.[2]

---

1. Luke 10 : 15-27.   2. John 11 : 55-57.

Jesus therefore six days before the passover came to Bethany, where Lazarus was, whom Jesus raised from the dead.[1]

The common people therefore of the Jews learned that he was there: and they came, not for Jesus' sake only, but that they might see Lazarus also, whom he had raised from the dead. But the chief priests took counsel that they might put Lazarus also to death; because that by reason of him many of the Jews went away, and believed on Jesus.[2]

Now when Jesus was in Bethany, in the house of Simon the leper,[3] they made him a supper there: and Martha served; but Lazarus was one of them that sat at meat with him. Mary therefore took[4] [an alabaster cruse of ointment of spikenard very costly; *and* she brake the cruse, and poured it over his head[5]] a pound of ointment of spikenard, very precious, and anointed the feet of Jesus, and wiped his feet with her hair: and the house was filled with the odour of the ointment.[6] But when the disciples saw it, they had indignation, saying, To what purpose[7] hath this waste of the ointment been made?[8] And they murmured against her.[9] But Judas Iscariot, one of his disciples, which should betray him, saith, Why was not this ointment sold for three hundred pence, and given to the poor? Now this he said, not because he cared for the poor; but because he was a thief, and having the bag took away what was put therein.[10] But Jesus perceiving it said unto them, Why trouble ye the woman? for she hath wrought a good work upon me. For ye have the poor always with you,[11] and whensoever ye will ye can do them good: but me ye have not always. She hath done what she could.[12] For in that she poured this ointment upon my body, she did it to prepare me for burial.[13] And verily I say unto you, Wheresoever this gospel shall be preached throughout the whole world, that also which this woman hath done shall be spoken of for a memorial of her.[14]

---

1. John 12 : 1.
2. John 12 : 9-11.
3. Matt. 26 : 6.
4. John 12 : 2, 3.
5. Mark 14 : 3.
6. John 12 : 3.
7. Matt. 26 : 8.
8. Mark 14 : 4.
9. Mark 14 : 5.
10. John 12 : 4-6.
11. Matt. 26 : 10, 11.
12. Mark 14 : 7, 8.
13. Matt. 26 : 12.
14. Mark 14 : 9.

§ 92—JESUS MAKES HIS TRIUMPHAL ENTRY INTO JERUSALEM.

And when he had thus spoken, he went on before, going up to Jerusalem.

And it came to pass, when he drew nigh unto Bethphage and Bethany, at the mount that is called *the mount* of Olives, he sent two of the disciples, saying, Go your way into the village over against *you* ; in the which as ye enter ye shall find a colt tied, whereon no man ever yet sat : loose him, and bring him. And if any one ask you, Why do ye loose him? thus shall ye say, The Lord hath need of him,[1] and straightway he will send him back hither. And they went away, and found a colt tied at the door without in the open street.[2] And as they were loosing the colt, the owners thereof said unto them, Why loose ye the colt?[3] And they said unto them even as Jesus had said : and they let them go. And they bring the colt unto Jesus, and cast on him their garments ;[4] and set Jesus thereon.[5]

On the morrow a great multitude that had come to the feast, when they heard that Jesus was coming to Jerusalem, took the branches of the palm trees, and went forth to meet him, and cried out, Hosanna : Blessed *is* he that cometh in the name of the Lord, even the King of Israel.[6]

Now this is come to pass, that it might be fulfilled which was spoken by the prophet, saying,

Tell ye the daughter of Zion,
Behold, thy King cometh unto thee,
Meek, and riding upon an ass,
And upon a colt the foal of an ass.[7]

And the most part of the multitude spread their garments in the way ; and others cut branches from the trees, and spread them in the way.[8]

And as he was now drawing nigh, *even* at the descent of

---

1. Luke 19 : 28-31.
2. Mark 11 : 3, 4.
3. Luke 19 : 33.
4. Mark 11 : 6, 7.
5. Luke 19 : 35.
6. John 12: 12, 13.
7. Matt. 21 : 4, 5.
8. Matt. 21 : 8.

9

the mount of Olives, the whole multitude of the disciples began to rejoice and praise God with a loud voice for all the mighty works which they had seen; saying, Blessed *is* the King that cometh in the name of the Lord : peace in heaven, and glory in the highest.[1]

These things understood not his disciples at the first : but when Jesus was glorified, then remembered they that these things were written of him, and that they had done these things unto him. The multitude therefore that was with him when he called Lazarus out of the tomb, and raised him from the dead, bare witness. For this cause also the multitude went and met him, for that they heard that he had done this sign. The Pharisees therefore said among themselves, Behold how ye prevail nothing : lo, the world is gone after him.[2]

§ 93—JESUS WEEPS OVER JERUSALEM.

And some of the Pharisees from the multitude said unto him, Master, rebuke thy disciples. And he answered and said, I tell you that, if these shall hold their peace, the stones will cry out.

And when he drew nigh, he saw the city and wept over it, saying, If thou hadst known in this day, even thou, the things which belong unto peace ! but now they are hid from thine eyes. For the days shall come upon thee, when thine enemies shall cast up a bank about thee, and compass thee around, and keep thee in on every side, and shall dash thee to the ground, and thy children within thee ; and they shall not leave in thee one stone upon another ; because thou knewest not the time of thy visitation.[3]

---

1. Luke 19: 37, 38. 2. John 12: 16-19. 3. Luke 19 : 39-44.

§ 94—THE MULTITUDES AND THE CHILDREN PRAISE THE LORD.

And when he was come into Jerusalem, all the city was stirred, saying, Who is this? And the multitudes said, This is the prophet, Jesus, from Nazareth of Galilee.[1]

And the blind and the lame came to him in the temple: and he healed them. But when the chief priests and the scribes saw the wonderful things that he did, and the children that were crying in the temple and saying, Hosanna to the son of David; they were moved with indignation, and said unto him, Hearest thou what these are saying? And Jesus saith unto them, Yea: did ye never read, Out of the mouth of babes and sucklings thou hast perfected praise?[2] and when he had looked round about upon all things, it being now eventide, he went out[3] of the city[4] unto Bethany with the twelve,[5] and lodged there.[6]

§ 95—THE BARREN FIG TREE AND THE SECOND PURGING OF THE TEMPLE.

And on the morrow, when they were come out from Bethany, he hungered. And seeing a fig tree afar off having leaves, he came, if haply he might find anything thereon: and when he came to it, he found nothing but leaves; for it was not the season of figs. And he answered and said unto it, No man eat fruit from thee henceforward for ever. And his disciples heard it.

And they come to Jerusalem: and he entered into the temple, and began to cast out them that sold and them that bought in the temple, and overthrew the tables of the money-changers, and the seats of them that sold the doves; and he would not suffer that any man should carry a vessel through the temple. And he taught, and said unto them,

---

1. Matt. 21 : 10, 11.   3. Mark 11 : 11.   5. Mark 11 : 11.
2. Matt. 21, 14-16.   4. Matt. 21 : 17.   6. Matt. 21 : 17.

Is it not written, My house shall be called a house of prayer for all the nations? but ye have made it a den of robbers.[1]

And he was teaching daily in the temple. But the chief priests and the scribes and the principal men of the people[2] heard it, and sought how they might destroy him: for they feared him, for all the multitude was astonished at his teaching.[3] And they could not find what they might do; for the people all hung upon him, listening.[4]

§ 96—JESUS FORETELLS HIS "LIFTING UP."

Now there were certain Greeks among those that went up to worship at the feast: these therefore came to Philip, which was of Bethsaida of Galilee, and asked him, saying, Sir, we would see Jesus. Philip cometh and telleth Andrew: Andrew cometh, and Philip, and they tell Jesus. And Jesus answereth them, saying, The hour is come, that the Son of man should be glorified. Verily, verily, I say unto you, Except a grain of wheat fall into the earth and die, it abideth by itself alone; but if it die, it beareth much fruit. He that loveth his life loseth it; and he that hateth his life in this world shall keep it unto life eternal. If any man serve me, let him follow me; and where I am, there shall also my servant be: if any man serve me, him will the Father honour. Now is my soul troubled; and what shall I say? Father, save me from this hour. But for this cause came I unto this hour. Father, glorify thy name. There came therefore a voice out of heaven, *saying*, I have both glorified it, and will glorify it again. The multitude therefore, that stood by, and heard it, said that it had thundered: others said, An angel hath spoken to him. Jesus answered and said, This voice hath not come for my sake, but for your sakes. Now is the judgement of this world: now shall the prince of this world be cast out. And I, if I be lifted up from the earth, will draw all men unto myself. But this he said, signifying by what manner of death he should die.[5]

---

1. Mark 11: 12-17.   3. Mark 11: 18.   5. John 12: 20-33.
2. Luke 19: 47.   4. Luke 19: 48.

The multitude therefore answered him, We have heard out
of the law that the Christ abideth for ever: and how sayest
thou, The Son of man must be lifted up? who is this Son of
man? Jesus therefore said unto them, Yet a little while is
the light among you. Walk while ye have the light, that
darkness overtake you not : and he that walketh in the
darkness knoweth not whither he goeth. While ye have
the light, believe on the light, that ye may become sons of
light.

These things spake Jesus, and he departed and hid himself from them. But though he had done so many signs
before them, yet they believed not on him : that the word of
Isaiah the prophet might be fulfilled, which he spake,

Lord, who hath believed our report?

And to whom hath the arm of the Lord been revealed?
For this cause they could not believe, for that Isaiah said
again,

He hath blinded their eyes, and he hardened their
heart ;

Lest they should see with their eyes, and perceive with
their heart,

And should turn,

And I should heal them.
These things said Isaiah, because he saw his glory ; and he
spake of him. Nevertheless even of the rulers many
believed on him ; but because of the Pharisees they did not
confess *it*, lest they should be put out of the synagogue : for
they loved the glory of men more than the glory of God.

And Jesus cried and said, He that believeth on me, believeth not on me, but on him that sent me. And he that
beholdeth me beholdeth him that sent me. I am come a
light into the world, that whosoever believeth on me may
not abide in the darkness And if any man hear my sayings,
and keep them not, I judge him not : for I came not to
judge the world, but to save the world. He that rejecteth
me, and receiveth not my sayings, hath one that judgeth
him : the word that I spake, the same shall judge him in the[1]

---

1. John 12 : 34-48.

last day. For I spake not from myself ; but the Father
which sent me, he hath given me a commandment, what I
should say, and what I should speak.   And I know that his
commandment is life eternal : the things therefore which I
speak, even as the Father hath said unto me, so I speak.[1]

§ 97—THE BARREN FIG TREE WITHERED.

And every evening he went forth out of the city.

And as they passed by in the morning, they saw the fig
tree withered away from the roots.[2]

And when the disciples saw it, they marvelled, saying,
How did the fig tree immediately wither away ?[3]

And Peter calling to remembrance saith unto him, Rabbi,
behold. the fig tree which thou cursedst is withered away.
And Jesus answering saith unto them, Have faith in God.
Verily I say unto you, Whosoever shall say unto this mountain, Be thou taken up and cast into the sea ; and shall not
doubt in his heart, but shall believe that what he saith cometh
to pass; he shall have it.   Therefore 1 say unto you, All
things whatsoever ye pray and ask for, believe that ye have
received them, and ye shall have them   And whensoever ye
stand praying, forgive, if ye have aught against any one ;
that your Father also which is in heaven may forgive you
your trespasses.[4]

And it came to pass, on one of the days, as he was teaching the people in the temple, and preaching the gospel, there
came upon him the chief priests and the scribes with the
elders ; and they spake, saying unto him, Tell us : By what
authority doest thou these things ? or who is he that gave
thee this authority ?   And he answered and said unto them,
I also will ask you a question,[5] which if ye tell me, I likewise will tell you by what authority I do these things.[6]   The
baptism of John, was it from heaven, or from men ?[7] answer
me.[8]   And they reasoned with themselves, saying, If we

---

1. John 12 : 48-50.
2. Mark 11 : 19, 20.
3. Matt. 21 : 20.
4. Mark 11 : 21-25.
5. Luke 20 : 1-3.
6. Matt. 21 : 24.
7. Luke 20 : 4.
8. Mark 11 : 31.

shall say, from heaven ; he will say, Why[1] then[2] did ye not believe him ? But if we shall say, From men ; all the people will stone us : for they be persuaded that John was a prophet. And they answered, that they knew not whence *it was.* And Jesus said unto them, Neither tell I you by what authority I do these things.[3]

§ 98—THE PARABLES OF THE TWO SONS, OF THE WICKED HUSBANDMEN AND THE VINEYARD, AND OF THE MARRIAGE FEAST.

But what think ye ? A man had two sons ; and he came to the first, and said, Son, go work to-day in the vineyard. And he answered and said, I will not : but afterward he repented himself, and went. And he came to the second, and said likewise. And he answered and said, I *go*, sir : and went not. Whether of the twain did the will of his father ? They say, The first. Jesus saith unto them, Verily I say unto you, that the publicans and the harlots go into the kingdom of God before you. For John came unto you in the way of righteousness, and ye believed him not : but the publicans and the harlots believed him : and ye, when ye saw it, did not even repent yourselves afterward, that ye might believe him.

Hear another parable : There was a man that was a householder, which planted a vineyard, and set a hedge about it, and digged a winepress in it, and built a tower, and let it out to husbandmen, and went into another country[4] for a long time.[5] And when the season of the fruits drew near, he sent his servants to the husbandmen, to receive[6] of the fruits of the vineyard. And they took him, and beat him, and sent him away empty. And again he sent unto them another servant ; and him they wounded in the head, and handled shamefully. And he sent another ; and him they killed : and many others ; beating some, and killing some.[7]

---

1. Luke 20 : 5.
2. Mark 11 : 31.
3. Luke 20 : 5-8.
4. Matt. 21 : 28-33.
5. Luke 20 : 9.
6. Matt. 21 : 34.
7. Mark 12 : 2-5.

And the lord of the vineyard said, What shall I do? I will
send my beloved son: it may be they will reverence him.
But when the husbandmen saw him, they reasoned one with
another, saying, This is the heir: let us kill him, that the
inheritance may be ours.[1]　And they took him, and cast him
forth out of the vineyard, and killed him.　When therefore
the lord of the vineyard shall come, what will he do unto
those husbandmen?　They say unto him, He will miserably
destroy those miserable men, and will let out the vineyard
unto other husbandmen, which shall render him the fruits
in their seasons.[2]　And when they heard it, they said, God
forbid.　But he looked upon them, and said,[3] Did ye never
read in the scriptures,

    The stone which the builders rejected,
    The same was made the head of the corner:
    This was from the Lord,
    And it is marvellous in our eyes?

Therefore say I unto you, the kingdom of God shall be taken
away from you, and shall be given to a nation bringing forth
the fruits thereof.　And he that falleth on this stone shall
be broken to pieces: but on whomsoever it shall fall, it will
scatter him as dust.　And when the chief priests and the
Pharisees heard his parables, they perceived that he spake
of them.[4]　And they sought to lay hold on him,[5] in that very
hour; and[6] they feared the multitudes, because they took
him for a prophet,[7] and they left him and went away.[8]

And Jesus answered and spake again in parables unto them,
saying, The kingdom of heaven is likened unto a certain
king, which made a marriage feast for his son, and sent forth
his servants to call them that were bidden to the marriage
feast: and they would not come.　Again he sent forth other
servants, saying, Tell them that are bidden, Behold, I have
made ready my dinner: my oxen and my fatlings are killed,
and all things are ready: come to the marriage feast.　But
they made light of it, and went their ways, one to his own

---

1. Luke 20: 13, 14.　　4. Matt. 21: 42-45.　　7. Matt. 21: 46.
2. Matt. 21: 39-41.　　5. Mark 12: 12.　　8. Mark 12: 12.
3. Luke 20: 16, 17.　　6. Luke 20: 19.

farm, another to his merchandise : and the rest laid hold on
his servants, and entreated them shamefully, and killed
them.   But the king was wroth ; and he sent his armies,
and destroyed those murderers, and burned their city.
Then saith he to his servants, The wedding is ready, but
they that were bidden were not worthy.   Go ye therefore
unto the partings of the highways, and as many as ye shall
find, bid to the marriage feast.   And those servants went
out into the highways, and gathered together all as many as
they found, both bad and good : and the wedding was filled
with guests.   But when the king came in to behold the
guests, he saw there a man which had not on a wedding
garment : and he saith unto him, Friend, how camest thou in
hither not having a wedding garment ?   And he was speech-
less.   Then the king said to the servants, Bind him hand
and foot, and cast him out into the outer darkness ; there
shall be the weeping and gnashing of teeth.   For many are
called, but few chosen.[1]

§ 99—JESUS REPLIES TO THE PHARISEES CONCERNING THE TRIBUTE MONEY, AND REVEALS THE STATE OF THE SAINTS IN HEAVEN.

Then went the Pharisees, and took counsel how they
might ensnare him in *his* talk.[2]   And they watched him, and
sent forth spies, which feigned themselves to be righteous,
that they might take hold of his speech, so as to deliver him
up to the rule, and to the authority of the governor.[3]   And
they send to him their disciples, with the Herodians, saying,
Master, we know that thou art true, and teachest the way of
God in truth, and carest not for any one : for thou regardest
not the person of men,[4] but of a truth teachest the way
of God.[5]   Tell us therefore, What thinkest thou ? Is it lawful to give tribute unto Cæsar, or not?[6]   Shall we give, or

---

1. Matt. 22 : 1-14.   3. Luke 20 : 20.   5. Luke 20 : 21.
2. Matt. 22 : 15.   4. Matt. 22 : 16.   6. Matt. 22 : 17.

shall we not give ?[1] But Jesus perceived their wickedness, and said, Why tempt ye me, ye hypocrites ? Shew me the tribute money. And they brought unto him a penny. And he saith unto them, Whose is this image and superscription ? They say unto him, Cæsar's. Then saith he unto them, Render therefore unto Cæsar the things that are Cæsar's ; and unto God the things that are God's.[2] And they were not able to take hold of the saying before the people : and they marvelled at his answer, and held their peace,[3] and left him, and went their way.

And on that day,[4] there came to him certain of the Sadducees, they which say that there is no resurrection ; and they asked him, saying, Master, Moses wrote unto us, that if a man's brother die, having a wife, and he be childless, his brother should take the wife, and raise up seed unto his brother.[5]

Now there were with us seven brethren : and the first married and deceased, and having no seed left his wife unto his brother ; in like manner the second also, and the third, unto the seventh. And after them all the woman died. In the resurrection therefore whose wife shall she be of the seven ? for they all had her. But Jesus answered and said unto them, Ye do err, not knowing the scriptures, nor the power of God.[6] The sons of this world marry, and are given in marriage : but they that are accounted worthy to attain to that world, and the resurrection from the dead, neither marry, nor are given in marriage : for neither can they die any more : for they are equal unto the angels ; and are sons of God, being sons of the resurrection.[7]

But as touching the dead, that they are raised ; have ye not read in the book of Moses, in *the place concerning* the Bush, how God spake unto him, saying, I *am* the God of Abraham, and the God of Isaac, and the God of Jacob ?[8] Now he is not the God of the dead, but of the living : for

---

1. Mark 12 : 14.   4. Matt. 22 : 22, 23.   7. Luke 20 : 34-36.
2. Matt. 22 : 18-21.   5. Luke 20 : 27, 28.   8. Mark 12 : 26.
3. Luke 20 : 26.   6. Matt. 22 : 25-29.

all live unto him.[1] Ye do greatly err.[2] And when the multitudes heard it, they were astonished at his teaching.[3] And certain of the scribes answering said, Master, thou hast well said. For they durst not any more ask him any question.[4]

§ 100—THE TWO GREAT COMMANDMENTS.

But the Pharisees, when they heard he had put the Sadducees to silence, gathered themselves together. And one of them, a lawyer, asked him a question, tempting him, Master, which is the great commandment in the law?[5] Jesus answered, The first is, Hear, O Israel ; The Lord our God, the Lord is one : and thou shalt love the Lord thy God with all thy heart, and with all thy soul, and with all thy mind, and with all thy strength.[6] This is the great and first commandment. And a second like *unto it* is this, Thou shalt love thy neighbour as thyself.[7] There is none other commandment greater than these.[8] On these two commandments hangeth the whole law, and the prophets.[9] And the scribe said unto him, Of a truth, Master, thou hast well said that he is one ; and there is none other but he : and to love him with all the heart, and with all the understanding, and with all the strength, and to love his neighbour as himself, is much more than all whole burnt offerings and sacrifices. And when Jesus saw that he answered discreetly, he said unto him, Thou art not far from the kingdom of God. And no man after that durst ask him any question.[10]

§ 101—JESUS SHEWS THAT THE CHRIST IS DAVID'S SON AND DAVID'S LORD.

Now while the Pharisees were gathered together, Jesus asked them a question, saying, What think ye of the Christ? whose son is he? They say unto him, *The son* of David.

---

1. Luke 20 : 38.
2. Mark 12 : 27.
3. Matt. 22 : 33.
4. Luke 20 : 39, 40.
5. Matt. 22 : 34-36.
6. Mark 12 : 29, 30.
7. Matt. 22 : 38, 39.
8. Mark 12 : 31.
9. Matt. 22 : 40.
10. Mark 12 : 32-34.

He saith unto them, How then doth David in the Spirit call
him Lord, saying,[1] in the book of Psalms,[2]

The Lord said unto my Lord,

Sit thou on my right hand,

Till I put thine enemies underneath thy feet ?

If David then calleth him Lord, how is he his son ?   And
no one was able to answer him a word, neither durst any
man from that day forth ask him any more questions.[3]   And
the common people heard him gladly.[4]

§ 102—JESUS WARNS HIS DISCIPLES AGAINST THE EXAMPLE OF THE SCRIBES AND PHARISEES AND LAMENTS OVER JERUSALEM.

Then spake Jesus to the multitudes and to his disciples,
saying, The scribes and the Pharisees sit on Moses' seat :
all things therefore whatsoever they bid you, *these* do and
observe : but do not ye after their works ; for they say, and
do not.   Yea, they bind heavy burdens and grievous to be
borne, and lay them on men's shoulders ; but they themselves will not move them with their finger.   But all their
works they do for to be seen of men : for they make broad
their phylacteries, and enlarge the borders *of their garments*,
and love the chief place at feasts, and the chief seats in the
synagogues, and[5] to walk in long robes and *to have*[6] salutations in the marketplaces, and to be called of men, Rabbi.
But be not ye called Rabbi : for one is your teacher, and all
ye are brethren.   And call no man your father on the earth:
for one is your Father, which is in heaven.   Neither be ye
called masters : for one is your master, *even* the Christ.
But he that is greatest among you shall be your servant.
And whosoever shall exalt himself shall be humbled ; and
whosoever shall humble himself shall be exalted.

But woe unto you, scribes and Pharisees, hypocrites !
because ye shut the kingdom of heaven against men : for ye

---

1. Matt. 22 : 43.   3. Matt. 22 : 44-46.   5. Matt. 23 : 1-6.
2. Luke 20 : 42.   4. Mark 12 : 37.   6. Mark 12 : 38.

enter not in yourselves, neither suffer ye them that are entering in to enter[1] [which devour widows' houses, and for a pretence make long prayers : these shall receive greater condemnation[2]].

Woe unto you, scribes and Pharisees, hypocrites ! for ye compass sea and land to make one proselyte ; and when he is become so, ye make him twofold more a son of hell than yourselves.

Woe unto you, ye blind guides, which say, Whosoever shall swear by the temple, it is nothing ; but whosoever shall swear by the gold of the temple, he is a debtor. Ye fools and blind : for whether is greater, the gold, or the temple that hath sanctified the gold ? And, Whosoever shall swear by the altar, it is nothing ; but whosoever shall swear by the gift that is upon it, he is a debtor. Ye blind : for whether is greater, the gift, or the altar that sanctifieth the gift ? He therefore that sweareth by the altar, sweareth by it, and by all things thereon. And he that sweareth by the temple, sweareth by it, and by him that dwelleth therein. And he that sweareth by the heaven, sweareth by the throne of God, and by him that sitteth thereon.

Woe unto you, scribes and Pharisees, hypocrites! for ye tithe mint and anise and cummin, and have left undone the weightier matters of the law, judgement, and mercy, and faith : but these ye ought to have done, and not to have left the other undone. Ye blind guides, which strain out the gnat, and swallow the camel.

Woe unto you, scribes and Pharisees, hypocrites! for ye cleanse the outside of the cup and of the platter, but within they are full from extortion and excess. Thou blind Pharisee, cleanse first the inside of the cup and of the platter, that the outside thereof may become clean also.

Woe unto you, scribes and Pharisees, hypocrites! for ye are like unto whited sepulchres, which outwardly appear beautiful, but inwardly are full of dead men's bones, and of all uncleanness. Even so ye also outwardly appear righteous unto men, but inwardly ye are full of hypocrisy and iniquity.[3]

---

1. Matt. 23 : 7-13.   2. Luke 20 : 47.   3. Matt.23 : 15-28.

Woe unto you, scribes and Pharisees, hypocrites! for ye build the sepulchres of the prophets, and garnish the tombs of the righteous, and say, If we had been in the days of our fathers, we should not have been partakers with them in the blood of the prophets. Wherefore ye witness to yourselves, that ye are sons of them that slew the prophets. Fill ye up then the measure of your fathers. Ye serpents, ye offspring of vipers, how shall ye escape the judgement of hell? Therefore, behold, I send unto you prophets, and wise men, and scribes: some of them shall ye kill and crucify; and some of them shall ye scourge in your synagogues, and persecute from city to city: that upon you may come all the righteous blood shed on the earth, from the blood of Abel the righteous unto the blood of Zachariah son of Barachiah, whom ye slew between the sanctuary and the altar. Verily I say unto you, All these things shall come upon this generation.

O Jerusalem, Jerusalem, which killeth the prophets, and stoneth them that are sent unto her! how often would I have gathered thy children together, even as a hen gathereth her chickens under her wings, and ye would not! Behold, your house is left unto you desolate. For I say unto you, Ye shall not see me henceforth, till ye shall say, Blessed *is* he that cometh in the name of the Lord.[1]

§ 103—THE WIDOW'S MITE.

And he sat down over against the treasury, and beheld how the multitude cast money into the treasury: and many that were rich cast in much. And there came a poor widow, and she cast in two mites, which make a farthing. And he called unto him his disciples, and said unto them, Verily I say unto you, This poor widow cast in more than all they which are casting into the treasury: for they all did cast in of their superfluity; but she of her want did cast in all that she had, *even* all her living.[2]

---

1. Matt. 23 : 29-39. 2. Mark 12 : 41-44.

§ 104—JESUS FORETELLS THE DESTRUCTION OF THE TEMPLE AND JERUSALEM, AND THE COMING OF THE SON OF MAN.

And Jesus went out from the temple, and was going on his way; and his disciples came to him to shew him the buildings of the temple.[1] And one of his disciples saith unto him, Master, behold, what manner of stones and what manner of buildings! And Jesus said unto him, Seest thou these great buildings?[2] Verily I say unto you,[3] As for these things which ye behold, the days will come, in which there shall not be left here one stone upon another, that shall not be thrown down.[4]

And as he sat on the mount of Olives over against the temple, Peter and James and John and Andrew asked him privately,[5] Master,[6] tell us, when shall these things be? and what *shall be* the sign when these things are all about to be accomplished?[7] [of thy coming and of the end of the world[8]]. And Jesus began to say unto them, Take heed that no man lead you astray. Many shall come in my name, saying, I am[9] the Christ;[10] and shall lead many astray. And when ye shall hear of wars and rumours of wars,[11] see that ye[12] be not troubled: *these things* must needs come to pass; but the end is not yet[13] [immediately[14]]. For nation shall rise against nation, and kingdom against kingdom: there shall be earthquakes in divers places; there shall be famines[15] and pestilences; and there shall be terrors and great signs from heaven.[16] These things are the beginning of travail.

But take ye heed to yourselves: for[17] before all these things, they shall lay their hands on you, and shall persecute you, delivering you up to the synagogues and prisons, bringing you before kings and governors for my name's

---

1. Matt. 24 : 1.	7. Mark 13 : 4.	13. Mark 13 ; 7.
2. Mark 13 : 1, 2.	8. Matt. 24 : 3.	14. Luke 21 : 9.
3. Matt. 24 : 2.	9. Mark 13 : 5, 6.	15. Mark 13 : 8.
4. Luke 21 : 6.	10. Matt. 24 : 5.	16. Luke 21 : 11.
5. Mark 13 : 3.	11. Mark 13 : 6, 7.	17. Mark 13 : 8, 9.
6. Luke 21 : 7.	12. Matt. 24 : 6.	

sake. It shall turn unto you for a testimony.[1] Then shall
they deliver you up unto tribulation, and shall kill you:
and ye shall be hated of all the nations for my name's sake.[2]
And the gospel must first be preached unto all the nations.
And when they lead you *to judgement*, and deliver you up,
be not anxious beforehand what ye shall speak: but whatsoever shall be given you in that hour, that speak ye: for it is
not ye that speak, but the Holy Ghost. And brother shall
deliver up brother to death, and the father his child; and
children shall rise up against parents, and cause them to be
put to death. And ye shall be hated of all men for my
name's sake.[3] Settle it therefore in your hearts, not to
meditate beforehand how to answer: for I will give you a
mouth and wisdom, which all your adversaries shall not be
able to withstand or to gainsay. But ye shall be delivered
up even by parents, and brethren, and kinsfolk, and friends;
and *some* of you shall they cause to be put to death. And
ye shall be hated of all men for my name's sake. And not
a hair of your head shall perish. In your patience ye shall
win your souls.[4]

And many false prophets shall arise, and shall lead many
astray. And because iniquity shall be multiplied, the love
of the many shall wax cold. But he that endureth to the end,
the same shall be saved. And this gospel of the kingdom
shall be preached in the whole world for a testimony unto
all the nations; and then shall the end come.

When therefore ye see the abomination of desolation,
which was spoken of by Daniel the prophet, standing in the
holy place (let him that readeth understand).[5]

[But when ye see Jerusalem compassed with armies, then
know that her desolation is at hand.] Then let them that
are in Judæa flee unto the mountains; and let them that
are in the midst of her depart out; and let not them that
are in the country enter therein;[6] and let him that is on the
housetop not go down, nor enter in, to take anything out of

---

1. **Luke 21 : 12, 13.**   3. **Mark 13 : 10-13.**   5. **Matt. 24 : 11-15.**
2. **Matt. 24 : 9.**   4. **Luke 21 : 14-19.**   6. **Luke 21 : 20, 21.**

his house : and let him that is in the field not return back to take his cloke.[1]

For these are days of vengeance, that all things which are written may be fulfilled. Woe unto them that are with child and to them that give suck in those days ![2]

And pray ye that your flight be not in the winter, neither on a sabbath : for then shall be great tribulation, such as has not been from the beginning of the[3] creation which God created until now, and never shall be. And except the Lord had shortened the days, no flesh would have been saved : but for the elect's sake, whom he chose, he shortened the days.[4]

For there shall be great distress upon the land, and wrath upon this people. And they shall fall by the edge of the sword, and shall be led captive into all the nations : and Jerusalem shall be trodden down of the Gentiles, until the times of the Gentiles be fulfilled.[5]

And then if any man shall say unto you, Lo, here is the Christ ; or, Lo, there ; believe *it* not : for there shall arise false Christs and false prophets, and shall shew[6] great[7] signs and wonders, that they may lead astray, if possible,[8] even[9] the elect. But take ye heed : behold, I have told you all things beforehand.[10]

If therefore they shall say unto you, Behold, he is in the wilderness ; go not forth : Behold, he is in the inner chambers ; believe *it* not. For as the lightning cometh forth from the east, and is seen even unto the west ; so shall be the coming of the Son of man. Wheresoever the carcase is, there will the eagles be gathered together.

But immediately, after the tribulation of those days, the sun shall be darkened, and the moon shall not give her light, and the stars shall fall from heaven.[11] And there shall be signs in sun and moon and stars ; and upon the earth distress of nations, in perplexity for the roaring of the sea and the billows ; men fainting for fear, and for expec-

---

1. Mark 13 : 15, 16.
2. Luke 21 : 22, 23.
3. Matt. 24 : 20, 21.
4. Mark 13 : 19, 20.
5. Luke 21 : 23, 24.
6. Mark 13 : 21, 22.
7. Matt. 24 : 24.
8. Mark 13 : 22.
9. Matt. 24 : 24.
10. Mark 13 : 22, 23.
11. Matt. 24 : 26-29.

10

tation of the things which are coming on the world: for the powers of the heavens shall be shaken,[1] and then shall appear the sign of the Son of man in heaven: and then shall all the tribes of the earth mourn, and they shall see the Son of man coming on the clouds of heaven with power and great glory.[2] And then shall he[3] send forth his angels with a great sound of a trumpet, and they shall gather together his elect from the four winds,[4] from the uttermost part of the earth to the uttermost part of heaven.[5]

But when these things begin to come to pass, look up, and lift up your heads; because your redemption draweth nigh.[6]

Now from the fig tree learn her parable: when her branch is now become tender, and putteth forth its leaves, ye know that the summer is nigh; even so ye also, when ye see all these things[7] coming to pass, know ye that the kingdom of God is nigh,[8] even at the doors. Verily I say unto you, This generation shall not pass away, until all these things be accomplished. Heaven and earth shall pass away: but my words shall not pass away. But of that day or that hour knoweth no one, not even the angels in heaven, neither the Son, but the Father[9] only.[10] And as were the days of Noah, so shall be the coming of the Son of man. For as in those days which were before the flood they were eating and drinking, marrying and giving in marriage, until the day that Noah entered into the ark, and they knew not until the flood came, and took them all away; so shall be the coming of the Son of man. Then shall two men be in the field; one is taken, and one is left: two women *shall be* grinding at the mill: one is taken, and one is left.[11]

But take heed to yourselves, lest haply your hearts be overcharged with surfeiting, and drunkenness, and cares of this life, and that day come on you suddenly as a snare: for so shall it come upon all them that dwell on the face of all the earth. But watch ye at every season, making suppli-

---

1. Luke 21: 25, 26.	5. Mark 13: 27.	9. Mark 13: 24-32.
2. Matt. 24: 30.	6. Luke 21: 28.	10. Matt. 24: 36.
3. Mark 13: 27.	7. Matt. 24: 32, 33.	11. Matt. 24: 37-41.
4. Matt. 24: 31.	8. Luke 21: 31.	

cation, that ye may prevail to escape all these things that shall come to pass, and to stand before the Son of man.[1]

Take ye heed, watch and pray: for ye know not when the time is. *It is as when a man, sojourning in another country,* having left his house, and given authority to his servants, to each one his work, commanded also the porter to watch. Watch therefore: for ye know not when the lord of the house cometh, whether at even, or at midnight, or at cock-crowing, or in the morning: lest coming suddenly he find you sleeping. And what I say unto you I say unto all, Watch.[2]

§ 105—THE PARABLES OF THE TEN VIRGINS AND OF THE FIVE TALENTS.

But know this, that if the master of the house had known in what watch the thief was coming, he would have watched, and would not have suffered his house to be broken through. Therefore be ye also ready: for in an hour that ye think not the Son of man cometh. Who then is the faithful and wise servant, whom his lord hath set over his household, to give them their food in due season? Blessed is that servant, whom his lord when he cometh shall find so doing. Verily I say unto you, that he will set him over all that he hath. But if that evil servant shall say in his heart, My lord tarrieth; and shall begin to beat his fellow-servants, and shall eat and drink with the drunken; the lord of that servant shall come in a day when he expecteth not, and in an hour when he knoweth not, and shall cut him asunder, and appoint his portion with the hypocrites: there shall be the weeping and gnashing of teeth.[3]

Then shall the kingdom of heaven be likened unto ten virgins, which took their lamps, and went forth to meet the bridegroom. And five of them were foolish, and five were wise. For the foolish, when they took their lamps, took no oil with them : but the wise took oil in their vessels with

---

1. Luke 21 : 34-36.   2. Mark 13 : 33-37.   3. Matt. 24 : 42-51.

their lamps. Now while the bridegroom tarried, they all slumbered and slept. But at midnight there is a cry, Behold, the bridegroom ! Come ye forth to meet him. Then all those virgins arose, and trimmed their lamps. And the foolish said unto the wise, Give us of your oil ; for our lamps are going out. But the wise answered, saying, Peradventure there will not be enough for us and you ; go ye rather to them that sell, and buy for yourselves. And while they went away to buy, the bridegroom came; and they that were ready went in with him to the marriage feast : and the door was shut. Afterward come also the other virgins, saying, Lord, Lord, open to us. But he answered and said, Verily I say unto you, I know you not. Watch therefore, for ye know not the day nor the hour.

For *it is* as *when* a man, going into another country, called his own servants, and delivered unto them his goods. And unto one he gave five talents, to another two, to another one ; to each according to his several ability ; and he went on his journey. Straightway he that received the five talents went and traded with them, and made other five talents. In like manner he also that *received* the two gained other two. But he that received the one went away and digged in the earth, and hid his lord's money. Now after a long time the lord of those servants cometh, and maketh a reckoning with them. And he that received the five talents came and brought other five talents, saying, Lord, thou deliveredst unto me five talents : lo, I have gained other five talents. His lord said unto him, Well done, good and faithful servant : thou hast been faithful over a few things, I will set thee over many things : enter thou into the joy of thy lord. And he also that *received* the two talents came and said, Lord, thou deliveredst unto me two talents : lo, I have gained other two talents. His lord said unto him, Well done, good and faithful servant ; thou hast been faithful over a few things, I will set thee over many things : enter thou into the joy of thy lord. And he also that had received the one talent came and said, Lord, I[1]

---

1. Matt. 25 : 1-24.

knew thee that thou art a hard man, reaping where thou didst not sow, and gathering where thou didst not scatter : and I was afraid, and went away and hid thy talent in the earth : lo, thou hast thine own. But his lord answered and said unto him, Thou wicked and slothful servant, thou knewest that I reap where I sowed not, and gather where I did not scatter ; thou oughtest therefore to have put my money to the bankers, and at my coming I should have received back mine own with interest. Take ye away therefore the talent from him, and give it unto him that hath the ten talents. For unto every one that hath shall be given, and he shall have abundance : but from him that hath not, even that which he hath shall be taken away. And cast ye out the unprofitable servant into the outer darkness : there shall be the weeping and gnashing of teeth.

But when the Son of man shall come in his glory, and all the angels with him, then shall he sit on the throne of his glory : and before him shall be gathered all the nations : and he shall separate them one from another, as the shepherd separateth the sheep from the goats ; and he shall set the sheep on his right hand, but the goats on the left. Then shall the King say unto them on his right hand, Come, ye blessed of my Father, inherit the kingdom prepared for you from the foundation of the world : for I was an hungred, and ye gave me meat : I was thirsty, and ye gave me drink : I was a stranger, and ye took me in : naked, and ye clothed me ; I was sick, and ye visited me : I was in prison, and ye came unto me. Then shall the righteous answer him, saying, Lord, when saw we thee an hungred, and fed thee ? or athirst, and gave thee drink ? And when saw we thee a stranger, and took thee in ? or naked, and clothed thee ? And when saw we thee sick, or in prison, and came unto thee ? And the King shall answer and say unto them, Verily I say unto you, Inasmuch as ye did it unto one of these my brethren, *even* these least, ye did it unto me. Then shall he say also unto them on the left hand, Depart from me, ye cursed, into the eternal fire which is prepared for the[1]

---

1. Matt. 25 : 24-41.

devil and his angels : for I was an hungred, and ye gave
me no meat : I was thirsty, and ye gave me no drink :
I was a stranger, and ye took me not in : naked, and ye
clothed me not ; sick, and in prison, and ye visited me
not.   Then shall they also answer, saying, Lord, when
saw we thee an hungred, or athirst, or a stranger, or naked,
or sick, or in prison, and did not minister unto thee ?   Then
shall he answer them, saying, Verily I say unto you, Inasmuch as ye did it not unto one of these least, ye did it not
unto me.   And these shall go away into eternal punishment :
but the righteous into eternal life.[1]

§ 106—THE CHIEF PRIESTS CONSPIRE WITH
JUDAS ISCARIOT.

And every day he was teaching in the temple ; and every
night he went out, and lodged in the mount that is called
the mount of Olives.   And all the people came early in the
morning to him in the temple, to hear him.[2]   Now the
feast of unleavened bread drew nigh, which is called the
Passover.[3]

And it came to pass, when Jesus had finished all these
words, he said unto his disciples, Ye know that after two
days the passover cometh, and the Son of man is delivered
up to be crucified.   Then were gathered together the chief
priests, and the elders of the people, unto the court of the
high priest, who was called Caiaphas ; and they took counsel
together that they might take Jesus by subtilty, and kill
him.   But they said, Not during the feast, lest a tumult
arise among the people.[4]

And Satan entered into Judas who was called Iscariot,
being of the number of the twelve.   And he went away, and
communed with the chief priests and captains, how he might
deliver him unto them,[5] and said, What are ye willing to
give me, and I will deliver him unto you?[6]   And they, when
they . heard it, were glad, and promised to give him

---

1. Matt. 25 : 41-46.   3. Luke 22 : 1.   5. Luke 22 : 3, 4.
2. Luke 21 : 37, 38.   4. Matt. 26 : 1-5.   6. Matt. 26 : 15.

money,[1] and he consented.[2] And they weighed unto him
thirty pieces of silver.* And from that time he sought
opportunity to deliver him *unto them*,[3] in the absence of the
multitude.[4]

§ 107—THE DISCIPLES PREPARE THE LAST SUPPER.

And on the first day of unleavened bread, when they
sacrificed the passover, his disciples say unto him, Where
wilt thou that we go and make ready that thou mayest eat
the passover?[5] And he sent Peter and John, saying, Go
and make ready for us the passover, that we may eat. And
they said unto him, Where wilt thou that we make ready?
And he said unto them, Behold, when ye are entered into
the city, there shall meet you a man bearing a pitcher of
water; follow him into the house whereinto he goeth. And
ye shall say unto the good man of the house, The Master
saith unto thee, Where is the guest-chamber, where I shall
eat the passover with my disciples?[6] And he will himself
shew you a large upper room furnished *and* ready: and there
make ready for us. And the disciples went forth, and came
into the city, and found as he had said unto them: and they
made ready the passover.[7]

§ 108—JESUS AND HIS DISCIPLES BEGIN THE LAST
SUPPER.

Now before the feast of the passover, Jesus knowing that
his hour was come that he should depart out of this world
unto the Father, having loved his own which were in the
world, he loved them unto the end.[8]

And when the hour was come, he sat down, and the
apostles with him. And he said unto them, With desire I

---

1. Mark 14 : 11.
2. Luke 22 : 6.
3. Matt. 26 : 15, 16.
4. Luke 22 : 6.
5. Mark 14 : 12.
6. Luke 22 : 8-11.
7. Mark 14 : 15, 16.
8. John 13 : 1.

* Equal to £3 10s. 8d., about $17.10, the legal value of a slave, if he were
killed by a beast.

have desired to eat this passover with you before I suffer:
for I say unto you, I will not eat it, until it be fulfilled in
the kingdom of God. And he received a cup, and when he
had given thanks, he said, Take this, and divide it among
yourselves: for I say unto you, I will not drink from henceforth of the fruit of the vine, until the kingdom of God shall
come.[1]

§ 109—JESUS WASHES HIS DISCIPLES' FEET.

And during supper, the devil having already put into the
heart of Judas Iscariot, Simon's *son*, to betray him, *Jesus,*
knowing that the Father had given all things into his
hands, and that he came forth from God, and goeth unto
God, riseth from supper, and layeth aside his garments; and
he took a towel, and girded himself. Then he poureth
water into the bason, and began to wash the disciples' feet,
and to wipe them with the towel wherewith he was girded.
So he cometh to Simon Peter. He saith unto him, Lord,
dost thou wash my feet? Jesus answered and said unto
him, What I do thou knowest not now; but thou shalt
understand hereafter. Peter saith unto him, Thou shalt
never wash my feet. Jesus answered him, If I wash thee
not, thou hast no part with me. Simon Peter saith unto
him, Lord, not my feet only, but also my hands and my
head. Jesus saith to him, He that is bathed needeth not
save to wash his feet, but is clean every whit: and ye are
clean, but not all. For he knew him that should betray
him; therefore said he, Ye are not all clean.

So when he had washed their feet, and taken his garments,
and sat down again, he said unto them, Know ye what I
have done to you? Ye call me, Master, and, Lord: and ye
say well; for so I am. If I then, the Lord and the Master,
have washed your feet, ye also ought to wash one another's
feet. For I have given you an example, that ye also should
do as I have done to you. Verily, verily, I say unto you,
A servant is not greater than his lord; neither one that is[2]

---

1. Luke 22 : 14-18.   2 John 13 : 2-16.

sent greater than he that sent him. If ye know these things, blessèd are ye if ye do them. I speak not of you all: I know whom I have chosen: but that the scripture may be fulfilled, He that eateth my bread lifted up his heel against me. From henceforth I tell you before it come to pass, that, when it is come to pass, ye may believe that I am *he.* Verily, verily, I say unto you, He that receiveth whomsoever I send receiveth me; and he that receiveth me receiveth him that sent me.[1]

§ 110—JESUS FORETELLS HIS BETRAYAL BY JUDAS AND HIS DENIAL BY PETER.

When Jesus had thus said, he was troubled in the spirit, and testified, and said. Verily, verily, I say unto you, that one of you shall betray me.[2] And they began to question among themselves, which of them it was that should do this thing,[3] doubting of whom he spake.[4] And they were exceeding sorrowful, and began to say unto him every one, Is it I, Lord? And he answered and said, He that dipped his hand with me in the dish, the same shall betray me. The Son of man goeth, even as it is written of him: but woe unto that man through whom the Son of man is betrayed! good were it for that man if he had not been born.[5] There was at the table reclining in Jesus' bosom one of his disciples, whom Jesus loved. Simon Peter therefore beckoneth to him, and saith unto him, Tell *us* who it is of whom he speaketh. .He leaning back, as he was, on Jesus' breast saith unto him, Lord, who is it? Jesus therefore answereth, He it is, for whom I shall dip the sop, and give it him. So when he had dipped the sop, he taketh and giveth it to Judas, *the son* of Simon Iscariot.[6] And Judas, which betrayed him, answered and said, Is it I, Rabbi? He saith unto him, Thou hast said.[7] And after the sop, then entered Satan into him. Jesus therefore saith unto him,

---

1. John 13 : 17-20.　　4. John 13 : 22.　　6. John 13 : 23-26.
2. John 13 : 21.　　　　5. Matt. 26 : 22-24.　7. Matt. 26 : 25.
3 Luke 22 : 23.

That thou doest, do quickly. Now no man at the table knew for what intent he spake this unto him. For some thought because Judas had the bag, that Jesus said unto him, Buy what things we have need of for the feast ; or, that he should give something to the poor. He then having received the sop went out straightway : and it was night. When therefore he was gone out, Jesus saith, Now is the Son of man glorified, and God is glorified in him ; and God shall glorify him in himself, and straightway shall he glorify him.[1]

And there arose also a contention among them, which of them is accounted to be greatest. And he said unto them, The kings of the Gentiles have lordship over them ; and they that have authority over them are called Benefactors. But ye *shall* not *be* so: but he that is the greater among you, let him become as the younger; and he that is chief, as he that doth serve. For whether is greater, he that sitteth at meat, or he that serveth ? is not he that sitteth at meat ? but I am in the midst of you as he that serveth. But ye are they which have continued with me in my temptations ; and I appoint unto you a kingdom, even as my Father appointed unto me, that ye may eat and drink at my table in my kingdom ; and ye shall sit on thrones judging the twelve tribes of Israel. Simon, Simon, behold, Satan asked to have you, that he might sift you as wheat : but I made supplication for thee, that thy faith fail not : and do thou, when once thou hast turned again, stablish thy brethren. And he said unto him, Lord, with thee I am ready to go both to prison and to death. And he said, I tell thee, Peter, the cock shall not crow this day, until thou shalt thrice deny that thou knowest me.

And he said unto them, When I sent you forth without purse, and wallet, and shoes, lacked ye anything ? And they said, Nothing. And he said unto them, But now, he that hath a purse, let him take it, and likewise a wallet : and he that hath none, let him sell his cloke, and buy a sword. For I say unto you, that this which is written must[2]

---

1. John 13 : 27-32.　　2. Luke 22 : 24-37.

be fulfilled in me, And he was reckoned with transgressors : for that which concerneth me hath fulfilment. And they said, Lord, behold, here are two swords. And he said unto them, It is enough.[1]

§ 111—THE INSTITUTION OF THE LORD'S SUPPER.

Matt. 26 : 26-29.	Mark 14 : 22-25.	Luke 22 : 19, 20.
And as they were eating, Jesus took bread, and blessed, and brake it; and he gave to the disciples, and said, Take, eat; this is my body. And he took a cup, and gave thanks, and gave to them, saying, Drink ye all of it; for this is my blood of the covenant, which is shed for many unto remission of sins. But I say unto you, I will not drink henceforth of this fruit of the vine, until that day when I drink it new with you in my Father's kingdom.	And as they were eating, he took bread, and when he had blessed, he brake it, and gave to them, and said, Take ye: this is my body. And he took a cup, and when he had given thanks, he gave to them: and they all drank of it. And he said unto them, This is my blood of the covenant, which is shed for many. Verily, I say unto you, I will no more drink of the fruit of the vine, until that day when I drink it new in the kingdom of God.	And he took bread, and when he had given thanks, he brake it, and gave to them, saying, This is my body which is given for you: this do in remembrance of me. And the cup in like manner after supper, saying, This cup is the new covenant in my blood, *even* that which is poured out for you.

---

1. Luke 22 : 37, 38.

§ 112—JESUS' FAREWELL DISCOURSE TO HIS DISCIPLES
AT THE LAST SUPPER.

Little children, yet a little while I am with you. Ye shall seek me: and as I said unto the Jews, Whither I go, ye cannot come; so now I say unto you. A new commandment I give unto you, that ye love one another; even as I have loved you, that ye also love one another. By this shall all men know that ye are my disciples, if ye have love one to another.

Simon Peter saith unto him, Lord, whither goest thou? Jesus answered, Whither I go, thou canst not follow me now; but thou shalt follow afterward. Peter saith unto him, Lord, why cannot I follow thee even now? I will lay down my life for thee. Jesus answereth, Wilt thou lay down thy life for me? Verily, verily, I say unto thee, The cock shall not crow, till thou hast denied me thrice.[1]

Let not your heart be troubled: ye believe in God, believe also in me. In my Father's house are many mansions; if it were not so, I would have told you; for I go to prepare a place for you. And if I go and prepare a place for you, I come again, and will receive you unto myself; that where I am, *there* ye may be also. And whither I go, ye know the way. Thomas saith unto him, Lord, we know not whither thou goest; how know we the way? Jesus saith unto him, I am the way, and the truth, and the life: no one cometh unto the Father, but by me. If ye had known me, ye would have known my Father also: from henceforth ye know him, and have seen him. Philip saith unto him, Lord, shew us the Father, and it sufficeth us. Jesus saith unto him, Have I been so long time with you, and dost thou not know me, Philip? he that hath seen me hath seen the Father; how sayest thou, Shew us the Father? Believest thou not that I am in the Father, and the Father in me? the words that I say unto you I speak not from myself: but the Father abiding in me doeth his works. Believe me that I am in the[2]

---

1. John 13: 33-38.   2. John 14: 1-11.

Father, and the Father in me: or else believe me for the very works' sake. Verily, verily, I say unto you, He that believeth on me, the works that I do shall he do also; and greater *works* than these shall he do; because I go unto the Father. And whatsoever ye shall ask in my name, that will I do, that the Father may be glorified in the Son. If ye shall ask me anything in my name, that will I do. If ye love me, ye will keep my commandments. And I will pray the Father, and he shall give you another Comforter, that he may be with you forever, *even* the Spirit of truth: whom the world cannot receive; for it beholdeth him not, neither knoweth him: ye know him, for he abideth with you, and shall be in you. I will not leave you desolate: I come unto you. Yet a little while, and the world beholdeth me no more; but ye behold me: because I live, ye shall live also. In that day ye shall know that I am in my Father, and ye in me, and I in you. He that hath my commandments, and keepeth them, he it is that loveth me: and he that loveth me shall be loved of my Father, and I will love him, and will manifest myself unto him. Judas (not Iscariot) saith unto him, Lord, What is come to pass that thou wilt manifest thyself unto us, and not unto the world? Jesus answered and said unto him, If a man love me, he will keep my word: and my Father will love him, and we will come unto him, and make our abode with him. He that loveth me not keepeth not my words: and the word which ye hear is not mine, but the Father's who sent me.

These things have I spoken unto you, while *yet* abiding with you. But the Comforter, *even* the Holy Spirit, whom the Father will send in my name, he shall teach you all things, and bring to your remembrance all that I said unto you. Peace I leave with you; my peace I give unto you: not as the world giveth, give I unto you. Let not your heart be troubled, neither let it be fearful. Ye heard how I said to you, I go away, and I come unto you. If ye loved me, ye would have rejoiced, because I go unto the Father: for the Father is greater than I. And now I have told you[1]

---

1. John 14: 11-29.

before it come to pass, that, when it is come to pass, ye may believe. I will no more speak much with you, for the prince of the world cometh: and he hath nothing in me; but that the world may know that I love the Father, and as the Father gave me commandment, even so I do. Arise, let us go hence.[1]

§ 113—JESUS CONTINUES HIS DISCOURSE ON THE WAY TO GETHSEMANE.

And when they had sung a hymn, they went out unto the mount of Olives.[2]

I am the true vine, and my Father is the husbandman. Every branch in me that beareth not fruit he taketh it away: and every *branch* that beareth fruit, he cleanseth it, that it may bear more fruit. Already ye are clean because of the word which I have spoken unto you. Abide in me, and I in you. As the branch cannot bear fruit of itself, except it abide in the vine; so neither can ye, except ye abide in me. I am the vine, ye are the branches: He that abideth in me, and I in him, the same beareth much fruit: for apart from me ye can do nothing. If a man abide not in me, he is cast forth as a branch, and is withered; and they gather them, and cast them into the fire, and they are burned. If ye abide in me, and my words abide in you, ask whatsoever ye will, and it shall be done unto you. Herein is my Father glorified, that ye bear much fruit: and so shall ye be my disciples. Even as the Father hath loved me, I also have loved you: abide ye in my love. If ye keep my commandments, ye shall abide in my love; even as I have kept my Father's commandments, and abide in his love. These things have I spoken unto you, that my joy may be in you, and *that* your joy may be fulfilled. This is my commandment, that ye love one another, even as I have loved you. Greater love hath no man than this, that a man lay down his life for his friends. Ye are my friends, if ye do the[3]

---

1. John 14 : 29-31.   2. Matt. 26 : 30.   3. John 15 : 1-14.

things which I command you. No longer do I call you
servants; for the servant knoweth not what his lord doeth:
but I have called you friends; for all things that I heard
from my Father I have made known unto you.   Ye did not
choose me, but I chose you, and appointed you, that ye
should go and bear fruit, and *that* your fruit should abide:
that whatsoever ye shall ask of the Father in my name, he
may give it you.   These things I command you, that ye may
love one another.   If the world hateth you, ye know that it
hath hated me before *it hated* you.   If ye were of the world,
the world would love its own: but because ye are not of the
world, but I chose you out of the world, therefore the
world hateth you.   Remember the word that I said unto
you, A servant is not greater than his lord.   If they persecuted me, they will also persecute you; if they kept my
word, they will keep yours also.   But all these things will
they do unto you for my name's sake, because they know
not him that sent me.   If I had not come and spoken unto
them, they had not had sin: but now they have no excuse
for their sin.   He that hateth me hateth my Father also.
If I had not done among them the works which none other
did, they had not had sin: but now have they both seen and
hated both me and my Father.   But *this cometh to pass*, that
the word may be fulfilled that is written in their law, They
hated me without a cause.   But when the Comforter is come,
whom I will send unto you from the Father, *even* the Spirit
of truth, which proceedeth from the Father, he shall bear
witness of me: and ye also bear witne-s, because ye have
been with me from the beginning.[1]
  These things have I spoken unto you, that ye should not
be made to stumble.   They shall put you out of the synagogues: yea, the hour cometh, that whosoever killeth you
shall think that he offereth service unto God.   And these
things will they do, because they have not known the Father, nor me.   But these things have I spoken unto you,
that when their hour is come, ye may remember them, how
that I told you.   And these things I said not unto you from[2]

---

1. John 15 : 14-27.   2. John 16 : 1-4.

the beginning, because I was with you.　But now I go unto him that sent me; and none of you asketh me, Whither goest thou?　But because I have spoken these things unto you, sorrow hath filled your heart.　Nevertheless I tell you the truth; It is expedient for you that I go away: for if I go not away, the Comforter will not come unto you; but if I go, I will send him unto you.　And he, when he is come, will convict the world in respect of sin, and of righteousness, and of judgement: of sin, because they believe not on me; of righteousness, because I go to the Father, and ye behold me no more; of judgement, because the prince of this world hath been judged.　I have yet many things to say unto you, but ye cannot bear them now.　Howbeit when he, the Spirit of truth, is come, he shall guide you into all the truth: for he shall not speak from himself; but what things soever he shall hear, *these* shall he speak: and he shall declare unto you the things that are to come.　He shall glorify me: for he shall take of mine, and shall declare *it* unto you.　All things whatsoever the Father hath are mine: therefore said I, that he taketh of mine, and shall declare *it* unto you.　A little while, and ye behold me no more; and again a little while, and ye shall see me.　*Some* of his disciples therefore said one to another, What is this that he saith unto us, A little while, and ye behold me not; and again a little while, and ye shall see me: and, Because I go to the Father?　They said therefore, What is this that he saith, A little while?　We know not what he saith.　Jesus perceived that they were desirous to ask him, and he said unto them, Do ye inquire among yourselves concerning this, that I said, A little while, and ye behold me not, and again a little while, and ye shall see me?　Verily, verily, I say unto you, that ye shall weep and lament, but the world shall rejoice: ye shall be sorrowful, but your sorrow shall be turned into joy.　A woman when she is in travail hath sorrow, because her hour is come: but when she is delivered of the child, she remembereth no more her anguish, for the joy that a man is born into the world.　And ye therefore now have sorrow: but I[1]

---

1. John 16: 4-22.

will see you again, and your heart shall rejoice, and your joy
no one taketh away from you. And in that day ye shall ask
me nothing. Verily, verily, I say unto you, If ye shall ask
anything of the Father, he will give it you in my name.
Hitherto have ye asked nothing in my name: ask, and ye
shall receive, that your joy may be fulfilled.

These things have I spoken unto you in proverbs: the
hour cometh, when I shall no more speak unto you in proverbs, but shall tell you plainly of the Father. In that day
ye shall ask in my name : and I say not unto you, that I
will pray the Father for you; for the Father himself loveth
you, because ye have loved me, and have believed that I
came forth from the Father. I came out from the Father,
and am come into the world: again, I leave the world, and
go unto the Father. His disciples say, Lo, now speakest
thou plainly, and speakest no proverb. Now know we that
thou knowest all things, and needest not that any man
should ask thee: by this we believe that thou camest forth
from God. Jesus answered them, Do ye now believe? Behold, the hour cometh, yea, is come, that ye shall be scattered, every man to his own, and shall leave me alone: and
yet I am not alone, because the Father is with me. These
things have I spoken unto you, that in me ye may have
peace. In the world ye have tribulation: but be of good
cheer; I have overcome the world.[1]

§ 114—THE INTERCESSORY PRAYER OF JESUS
FOR HIS DISCIPLES.

These things spake Jesus; and lifting up his eyes to
heaven, he said, Father, the hour is come; glorify thy Son,
that the Son may glorify thee: even as thou gavest him
authority over all flesh, that whatsoever thou hast given
him, to them he should give eternal life. And this is life
eternal, that they should know thee the only true God, and
him whom thou didst send, *even* Jesus Christ. I glorified

---

1. John 16 : 22-33.

thee on the earth, having accomplished the work which thou
hast given me to do. And now, O Father, glorify thou me
with thine own self with the glory which I had with thee
before the world was. I manifested thy name unto the men
whom thou gavest me out of the world: thine they were,
and thou gavest them to me; and they have kept thy word.
Now they know that all things whatsoever thou hast given
me are from thee: for the words which thou gavest me I
have given unto them; and they received *them*, and knew of
a truth that I came forth from thee, and they believed that
thou didst send me. I pray for them: I pray not for the
world, but for those whom thou hast given me; for they are
thine: and all things that are mine are thine, and thine are
mine: and I am glorified in them. And I am no more in
the world, and these are in the world, and I come to thee.
Holy Father, keep them in thy name which thou hast given
me, that they may be one, even as we *are*. While I was
with them, I kept them in thy name which thou hast given
me: and I guarded them, and not one of them perished,
but the son of perdition; that the scripture might be fulfilled. But now I come to thee; and these things I speak
in the world, that they may have my joy fulfilled in themselves. I have given them thy word; and the world hated
them, because they are not of the world, even as I am not
of the world. I pray not that thou shouldest take them
from the world, but that thou shouldest keep them from the
evil *one*. They are not of the world, even as I am not of the
world. Sanctify them in the truth: thy word is truth. As
thou didst send me into the world, even so sent I them into
the world. And for their sakes I sanctify myself, that they
themselves also may be sanctified in truth. Neither for
these only do I pray, but for them also that believe on me
through their word; that they may all be one; even as thou,
Father, *art* in me, and I in thee, that they also may be in
us: that the world may believe that thou didst send me.
And the glory which thou hast given me I have given unto
them; that they may be one, even as we *are* one; I in them,[1]

---

1. John 17 : 1-23.

and thou in me, that they may be perfected into one; that the world may know that thou didst send me, and lovedst them, even as thou lovedst me. Father, that which thou hast given me, I will that, where I am, they also may be with me; that they may behold my glory, which thou hast given me: for thou lovedst me before the foundation of the world. O righteous Father, the world knew thee not, but I knew thee; and these knew that thou didst send me; and I made known unto them thy name, and will make it known; that the love wherewith thou lovedst me may be in them.[1]

§ 115—THE AGONY IN THE GARDEN.

When Jesus had spoken these words,[2] [and when they had sung a hymn][3] he went forth with his disciples over the brook Kidron,[4] unto the Mount of Olives.

Then saith Jesus unto them, All ye shall be offended in me this night: for it is written, I will smite the shepherd, and the sheep of the flock shall be scattered abroad. But after I am raised up, I will go before you into Galilee. But Peter answered and said unto him, If all shall be offended in thee, I will never be offended.[5] And Jesus saith unto him, Verily I say unto thee, that thou to-day, *even* this night, before the cock crow twice, shalt deny me thrice. But[6] Peter[7] spake exceeding vehemently,[8] Even[9] if I must die with thee, I will not deny thee. And in like manner also said[10] all the disciples.[11]

And they come unto a place[12] where was a garden,[13] which was named Gethsemane: and he [Jesus] saith unto his disciples, Sit ye here, while I[14] go yonder and[15] pray. And he taketh with him Peter and James and John, and began to be greatly amazed, and sore troubled. And he saith unto them, My soul is exceeding sorrowful even unto death:

---

1. John 17 : 23-26.
2. John 18 : 1.
3. Matt. 26 : 30.
4. John 18 : 1.
5. Matt. 26 : 30-33.
6. Mark 14 : 30, 31.
7. Matt. 26 : 35.
8. Mark 14 : 31.
9. Matt. 26 : 35.
10. Mark 14 : 31.
11. Matt. 26 : 35.
12. Mark 14 : 32.
13. John 18 : 1.
14. Mark 14 : 32, 33.
15. Matt. 26 : 36.

abide ye here, and watch[1] with me.[2] Pray that ye enter not into temptation.[3] And he went forward a little,[4] about a stone's cast,[5] and fell on the ground, and prayed that, if it were possible, the hour might pass away from him. And he said, Abba, Father, all things are possible unto thee;[6] if *thou* be willing,[7] remove this cup from me: howbeit not what I will, but what thou wilt.[8] And there appeared unto him an angel from heaven, strengthening him. And being in an agony he prayed more earnestly; and his sweat became as it were great drops of blood falling down upon the ground. And when he rose up from his prayer, he came unto the disciples, and found them sleeping for sorrow, and said[9] unto Peter, Simon, sleepest thou?[10] What, could ye not watch with me one hour? Watch and pray, that ye enter not into temptation: the spirit indeed is willing, but the flesh is weak. Again a second time he went away, and prayed, saying, O my Father, if this cannot pass away, except I drink it, thy will be done.[11]

And again he came, and found them sleeping, for their eyes were very heavy; and they wist not what to answer him.[12] And he left them again, and went away, and prayed a third time, saying again the same words. Then cometh he[13] the third time[14] to the disciples, and saith unto them, Sleep on now, and take your rest,[15] *it is* enough:[16] behold, the hour is at hand, and the Son of man is betrayed unto the hands of sinners. Arise, let us be going: behold, he is at hand that betrayeth me.[17]

---

1. Mark 14 : 33, 34.	7. Luke 22 : 42.	13. Matt. 26 : 44, 45.
2. Matt. 25 : 38.	8. Mark 14 : 36.	14. Mark 14 : 41.
3. Luke 22 : 40.	9. Luke 22 : 43-46.	15. Matt. 26 : 45.
4. Mark 14 : 35.	10. Mark 14 : 37.	16. Mark 14 : 41.
5. Luke 22 : 41.	11. Matt. 26 : 40-42.	17. Matt. 26 : 45, 46.
6. Mark 14 : 35-36.	12. Mark 14 : 40.	

§ 116—JESUS BETRAYED BY JUDAS ISCARIOT AND DESERTED BY THE DISCIPLES.

[He went forth with his disciples over the brook Kidron, where was a garden, into the which he entered, himself and his disciples.]

Now Judas also, which betrayed him, knew the place: for Jesus oft-times resorted thither with his disciples. Judas then, having received the band *of soldiers*, and officers from the chief priests and the Pharisees, cometh thither with lanterns and torches and weapons.[1]

[And straightway, while he yet spake, cometh Judas, one of the twelve, and with him a multitude with swords and staves, from the chief priests and the scribes and the elders.][2]

Jesus therefore, knowing all the things that were coming upon him, went forth, and saith unto them, Whom seek ye? They answered him, Jesus of Nazareth. Jesus saith unto them, I am *he*. And Judas also, which betrayed him, was standing with them. When therefore he said unto them, I am *he*, they went backward, and fell to the ground. Again therefore he asked them, Whom seek ye? And they said, Jesus of Nazareth. Jesus answered, I told you that I am *he*: if therefore ye seek me, let these go their way: that the word might be fulfilled which he spake, Of those whom thou hast given me I lost not one.[3]

Now he that betrayed him had given them a token, saying, Whomsoever I shall kiss, that is he; take him, and lead him away safely. And when he was come, straightway he came to him, and saith, Rabbi; and kissed him.[4] But Jesus said unto him, Judas, betrayest thou the Son of man with a kiss?[5] Friend, do that for which thou art come.[6]

So the band and the chief captain, and the officers of the Jews, seized Jesus and bound him.[7] And when they that

---

1. John 18: 1-3.   4. Mark 14: 44, 45.   6. Matt. 26: 50.
2. Mark 14: 43.   5. Luke 22: 48.   7. John 18: 12.
3. John 18: 4-9.

were about him saw what would follow, they said, Lord, shall we smite with the sword?[1] And behold, one of them that were with Jesus stretched out his hand, and drew his sword, and smote the servant of the high priest, and struck off his ear.[2] But Jesus answered and said, Suffer ye thus far. And he touched his ear, and healed him.[3]

Matt. 26 : 52-54.	John 18 : 10, 11.
Then saith Jesus unto him, Put up again thy sword into its place : for all they that take the sword shall perish with the sword. Or thinkest thou that I cannot beseech my Father, and he shall even now send me more than twelve legions of angels? How then should the scriptures be fulfilled, that thus it must be?	Simon Peter therefore having a sword drew it, and struck the high priest's servant, and cut off his right ear. Now the servant's name was Malchus. Jesus therefore said unto Peter, Put up the sword into the sheath : the cup which the Father hath given me, shall I not drink it?

Matt. 26 : 55, 56.	Luke 22 : 52, 53.
In that hour said Jesus to the multitudes, Are ye come out as against a robber with swords and staves to seize me? I sat daily in the temple teaching, and ye took me not. But all this is come to pass, that the scriptures of the prophets might be fulfilled.	And Jesus said unto the chief priests, and captains of the temple, and elders, which were come against him, Are ye come out, as against a robber, with swords and staves? When I was daily with you in the temple, ye stretched not forth your hands against me : but this is your hour, and the power of darkness.

Then all the disciples left him and fled.[4] And a certain young man followed with him, having a linen cloth cast about him, over *his* naked *body :* and they lay hold on him ; but he left the linen cloth, and fled naked.[5]

---

1. Luke 22 : 49.   3. Luke 22 : 51.   5. Mark 14 : 51, 52.
2. Matt. 26 : 51.   4. Matt. 26 : 56.

§ 117—JESUS IS ARRAIGNED BEFORE ANNAS IN THE HOUSE OF CAIAPHAS.

Matt. 26: 57.	John 18: 12, 13.
And they that had taken Jesus led him away to *the house of* Caiaphas the high priest, where the scribes and the elders were gathered together.	So the band and the chief captain, and the officers of the Jews, seized Jesus and bound him and led him to Annas first; for he was father in law to Caiaphas, which was high priest that year.

Now Caiaphas was he which gave counsel to the Jews, that it was expedient that one man should die for the people.[1]

The high priest therefore asked Jesus of his disciples, and of his teaching. Jesus answered him, I have spoken openly to the world; I ever taught in synagogues, and in the temple, where all the Jews come together; and in secret spake I nothing. Why askest thou me? ask them that have heard *me*, what I spake unto them: behold, these know the things which I said. And when he had said this, one of the officers standing by struck Jesus with his hand, saying, Answerest thou the high priest so? Jesus answered him, If I have spoken evil, bear witness of the evil: but if well, why smitest thou me? Annas therefore sent him bound unto Caiaphas the high priest.[2]

---

1. John 18: 14.   2. John 18: 19-24.

§118 —JESUS IS ARRAIGNED BEFORE CAIAPHAS, AND IS CONDEMNED.

Now the chief priests and the whole council sought[1] false[2] witness against Jesus to put him to death ; and found it not. For many bare false witness against him, and their witness agreed not together.   And there stood up certain, and bare false witness against him, saying, We heard him say, I will destroy this temple that is made with hands, and in three days I will build another, made without hands.   And not even so did their witness agree together.[3]

[But afterward came two, and said, This man said, I am able to destroy the temple of God, and to build it in three days.[4]]

And the high priest stood up in the midst, and asked Jesus, saying, Answerest thou nothing ? what is it which these witness against thee ? But he held his peace, and answered nothing. Again the high priest asked him, and saith unto him,[5] I adjure thee by the living God, that thou tell us whether thou be the Christ, the Son of God[6] [Son of the Blessed[7]]. Jesus saith unto him, Thou hast said : nevertheless I say unto you, Henceforth ye shall see the Son of man sitting at the right hand of power, and coming on the clouds of heaven.   Then the high priest rent his garments, saying, He hath spoken blasphemy : what further need have we of witnesses ? behold, now ye have heard the blasphemy : what think ye ? And they all condemned him to be worthy of death.[9]

---

1. Mark 14 : 55.
2. Matt. 26 : 59.
3. Mark 14 : 55-59.
4. Matt. 26 : 60, 61.
5. Mark 14 : 60, 61.
6. Matt. 26 : 63.
7. Mark 14 : 61.
8. Matt. 26 : 64-66.
9. Mark 14 : 64.

§ 119—THE DENIAL OF JESUS BY PETER.*

Now Peter was sitting without in the court : and a maid came unto him, saying, Thou also wast with Jesus the.Galilæan. But he denied before them all, saying, I know not what thou sayest. And when he was gone out into the porch, another *maid* saw him, and saith unto them that were there, This man also was with Jesus the Nazarene. And again he denied with an oath, I know not the man. And after a little while they that stood by came and said to Peter, Of a truth thou also art *one* of them ; for thy speech bewrayeth thee. Then began he to curse and to swear, I know not the man. And straightway the cock crew. And Peter remembered the word which Jesus had said, Before the cock crow, thou shalt deny me thrice. And he went out, and wept bitterly.[1]

And Peter had followed him afar off, even within, into the court of the high priest ; and he was sitting with the officers, and warming himself in the light *of the fire.*[2]

And as Peter was beneath in the court, there cometh one of the maids of the high priest ; and seeing Peter warming himself, she looked upon him, and saith, Thou also wast with the Nazarene, *even* Jesus. But he denied, saying, I neither know, nor understand what thou sayest : and he went out into the porch ; and the cock crew. And the maid saw him, and began again to say to them that stood by, This is *one* of them. But he again denied it. And after a little while again they that stood by said to Peter, of a truth thou art *one* of them ; for thou art a Galilæan. But he began to curse, and to swear, I know not this man of whom ye speak. And straightway the second time the cock crew. And Peter called to mind the word, how that Jesus said unto him, Before the cock crow twice, thou shalt deny me thrice, and when he thought thereon, he wept.[3]

---

* We give the four accounts of this in full.

1. Matt. 26 : 69-75.   2. Mark 14 : 54.   3. Mark 14: 66-72.

And when they had kindled a fire in the midst of the court, and had sat down together, Peter sat in the midst of them. And a certain maid seeing him as he sat in the light *of the fire,* and looking stedfastly upon him, said, This man also was with him. But he denied, saying, Woman, I know him not. And after a little while another saw him, and said, Thou also art *one* of them. But Peter said, Man, I am not. And after the space of about one hour another confidently affirmed, saying, Of a truth this man also was with him : for he is a Galilæan. But Peter said, Man, I know not what thou sayest. And immediately, while he yet spake, the cock crew. And the Lord turned, and looked upon Peter. And Peter remembered the word of the Lord, how that he said unto him, Before the cock crow this day, thou shalt deny me thrice. And he went out, and wept bitterly.[1]

And Simon Peter followed Jesus, and *so did* another disciple. Now that disciple was known unto the high priest, and entered in with Jesus into the court of the high priest; but Peter was standing at the door without. So the other disciple, which was known unto the high priest, went out and spake unto her that kept the door, and brought in Peter. The maid therefore that kept the door saith unto Peter, Art thou also *one* of this man's disciples? He saith, I am not. Now the servants and the officers were standing *there,* having made a fire of coals; for it was cold; and they were warming themselves: and Peter also was with them, standing and warming himself.[2]

Now Simon Peter was standing and warming himself. They said therefore unto him, Art thou also *one* of his disciples? He denied, and said, I am not. One of the servants of the high priest, being a kinsman of him whose ear Peter cut off, saith, Did not I see thee in the garden with him? Peter therefore denied again : and straightway the cock crew.[3]

---

1. Luke 22 : 55-62.   2. John 18 : 15 18.   3. John 18 : 25-27.

§ 120—JESUS IS MOCKED AND BEATEN, AND BROUGHT BEFORE THE HIGH COUNCIL.

Matt. 26 : 67, 68 ; 27 : 1, 2.

Then did they spit in his face and buffet him: and some smote him with the palms of their hands, saying, Prophesy unto us, thou Christ: who is he that struck thee? [And the officers received him with blows of their hands.[1]]

Now when morning was come, all the chief priests and the elders of the people took counsel against Jesus to put him to death: and they bound him, and led him away, and delivered him up to Pilate the governor.

Luke 22 : 63-71.

And the men that held *Jesus* mocked him, and beat him. And they blindfolded him, and asked him, saying, Prophesy: who is he that struck thee? And many other things spake they against him, reviling him.

And as soon as it was day, the assembly of the elders of the people was gathered together, both chief priests and scribes; and they led him away into their council, saying, If thou art the Christ, tell us. But he said unto them, If I tell you, ye will not believe: and if I ask *you*, ye will not answer. But from henceforth shall the Son of man be seated at the right hand of the power of God. And they all said, Art thou then the Son of God? And he said unto them, Ye say that I am. And they said, What further need have we of witness? for we ourselves have heard from his own mouth.

---

1. Mark 14 : 65.

And the whole company of
them rose up, and brought
him before Pilate,[1] [from Caiaphas into the palace: and it
was early[2]].

§ 121—THE REMORSE AND DEATH OF JUDAS.

Then Judas, which betrayed him, when he saw that he
was condemned, repented himself, and brought back the
thirty pieces of silver to the chief priests and elders, saying,
I have sinned in that I betrayed innocent blood.   But they
said, What is that to us? see thou *to it*.   And he cast down
the pieces of silver into the sanctuary, and departed; and
he went away and hanged himself.   And the chief priests
took the pieces of silver, and said, It is not lawful to put
them into the treasury, since it is the price of blood.   And
they took counsel, and bought with them the potter's field,
to bury strangers in.   Wherefore that field was called, The
field of blood, unto this day.   Then was fulfilled that which
was spoken by Jeremiah the prophet, saying, And they took
the thirty pieces of silver, the price of him that was priced,
whom *certain* of the children of Israel did price; and they
gave them for the potter's field, as the Lord appointed me.[3]

§ 122—PILATE EXAMINES JESUS, DECLARES HIS IN-
NOCENCE, AND SENDS HIM FOR TRIAL TO
HEROD.

They lead Jesus therefore from Caiaphas into the palace:
and it was early; and they themselves entered not into the
palace, that they might not be defiled, but might eat the
passover.   Pilate therefore went out unto them, and saith,
What accusation bring ye against this man?   They answered
and said unto him, If this man were not an evil-doer, we
should not have delivered him up unto thee.[4]   [And they

---

1. Luke 23: 1.   3. Matt. 27: 3-10.   4. John 18: 28-30.
2. John 18: 28.

began to accuse him, saying, We found this man perverting our nation, and forbidding to give tribute to Cæsar, and saying that he himself is Christ a king.[1]] Pilate therefore said unto them, Take him yourselves, and judge him according to your law. The Jews said unto him, It is not lawful for us to put any man to death: that the word of Jesus might be fulfilled, which he spake, signifying by what manner of death he should die.

Pilate therefore entered again into the palace, and called Jesus.[2]

Now Jesus stood before the governor: and the governor asked him, saying, Art thou the King of the Jews?[3] Jesus answered, Sayest thou this of thyself, or did others tell it thee concerning me? Pilate answered, Am I a Jew? Thine own nation and the chief priests delivered thee unto me: what hast thou done? Jesus answered, My kingdom is not of this world: if my kingdom were of this world, then would my servants fight, that I should not be delivered to the Jews: but now is my kingdom not from hence. Pilate therefore said unto him, Art thou a king then? Jesus answered, Thou sayest that I am a king. To this end have I been born, and to this end am I come into the world, that I should bear witness unto the truth. Every one that is of the truth heareth my voice. Pilate saith unto him, What is truth?

And when he had said this, he went out again unto the Jews.[4]

And Pilate said unto the chief priests and the multitudes, I find no fault in this man[5] [I find no crime in him[6]]. And the chief priests accused him of many things[7] [and] he answered nothing. Then saith Pilate unto him, Hearest thou not how many things they witness against thee? And he gave him no answer, not even to one word: insomuch that the governor marvelled greatly.[8] But they were the more urgent, saying, He stirreth up the people, teaching throughout all Judæa, and beginning from Galilee even unto

---

1. Luke 23 : 2.
2. John 18 : 31-33.
3. Matt. 27 : 11.
4. John 18 : 34-38.
5. Luke 23 : 4.
6. John 18 : 38.
7. Mark 15 : 3.
8. Matt. 27 : 12-14.

this place. But when Pilate heard it, he asked whether the man were a Galilæan. And when he knew that he was of Herod's jurisdiction, he sent him unto Herod, who himself also was at Jerusalem in these days.

Now when Herod saw Jesus, he was exceeding glad: for he was of a long time desirous to see him, because he had heard concerning him; and he hoped to see some miracle done by him. And he questioned him in many words; but he answered him nothing. And the chief priests and the scribes stood, vehemently accusing him. And Herod with his soldiers set him at nought, and mocked him, and arraying him in gorgeous apparel sent him back to Pilate. And Herod and Pilate became friends with each other that very day; for before they were at enmity between themselves.[1]

§ 123—THE JEWS REJECT JESUS AND CHOOSE BARABBAS.

Now at the feast the governor was wont to release unto the multitude one prisoner, whom they would. And they had then a notable prisoner called Barabbas,[2] *lying* bound with them that had made insurrection, men who in the insurrection had committed murder. And the multitude went up and began to ask him *to do* as he was wont to do unto them.[3]

And Pilate called together the chief priests and the rulers and the people, and said unto them, Ye brought unto me this man, as one that perverteth the people: and behold, I, having examined him before you, found no fault in this man touching those things whereof ye accuse him; no, nor yet Herod: for he sent him back unto us; and behold, nothing worthy of death hath been done by him. I will therefore chastise him, and release him.[4] But ye have a custom, that I should release unto you one at the passover: will ye therefore that I release unto you[5] Barabbas, or Jesus, which is

---

1. Luke 23 : 5-12.   3. Mark 15 : 7, 8.   5. John 18 : 39.
2. Matt. 27: 15, 16.   4. Luke 23 : 13-16.

called Christ,[1] the King of the Jews? For he perceived that
for envy the chief priests had delivered him up.[2] And while
he was sitting on the judgement-seat, his wife sent unto him,
saying, have thou nothing to do with that righteous man:
for I have suffered many things this day in a dream because
of him. Now the chief priests and the elders persuaded the
multitudes that they should ask for. Barabbas, and destroy
Jesus. But the governor answered and said unto them,
Whether of the twain will ye that I release unto you? And
they said, Barabbas.[3] But they cried out all together, saying, Away with this man, and release unto us Barabbas: one
who for a certain insurrection made in the city, and for
murder, was cast into prison.[4]

§ 124—THE SOLDIERS MOCK JESUS, AND THE JEWS DEMAND HIS CRUCIFIXION.

Then Pilate therefore took Jesus, and scourged him. And
the soldiers plaited a crown of thorns, and put it on his head,
and arrayed him in a purple garment; and they came unto
him, and said, Hail, King of the Jews! and they struck him
with their hands. And Pilate went out again, and saith
unto them, Behold, I bring him out to you, that ye may
know that I find no crime in him. Jesus therefore came
out, wearing the crown of thorns and the purple garment.
And *Pilate* saith unto them, Behold, the man![5]

Matt. 27 : 22, 23.	Mark 15 : 12-14.	Luke 23 : 20-23.
Pilate saith unto them, What then shall I do unto Jesus which is called Christ? They all say, Let him be crucified. And he said, Why, what	And Pilate again answered and said unto them, What then shall I do unto him whom ye call the King of the Jews? And they cried out again,	And Pilate spake unto them again, desiring to release Jesus; but they shouted, saying, Crucify, crucify him. And [Pilate] said unto them the

1. Matt. 27 : 17.   3. Matt. 27 : 19-21.   5. John 19 : 1-5.
2. Mark 15 : 9, 10.   4. Luke 23 : 18, 19.

evil hath he done ?
But they cried out
exceedingly, say-
ing, Let him be
crucified.

Crucify him. And
Pilate said unto
them, Why, what
evil hath he done ?
But they cried out
exceedingly, Cruci-
fy him.

third time, Why,
what evil hath this
man done ? I have
found no cause of
death in him : I will
therefore chastise
him, and release
him. But they were
instant with loud
voices, asking that
he might be cruci-
fied.

When therefore the chief priests and the officers saw him,
they cried out, saying, Crucify *him*, crucify *him*. Pilate
saith unto them, Take him yourselves, and crucify him : for
I find no crime in him. The Jews answered him, We have
a law, and by that law he ought to die, because he made
himself the Son of God. When Pilate therefore heard this
saying, he was the more afraid ; and he entered into the
palace again, and saith unto Jesus, Whence art thou ? But
Jesus gave him no answer. Pilate therefore saith unto him,
Speakest thou not unto me ? knowest thou not that I have
power to release thee, and have power to crucify thee ?
Jesus answered him, Thou wouldest have no power against
me, except it were given thee from above : therefore he that
delivered me unto thee hath greater sin.[1]

§ 125—PILATE DELIVERS JESUS TO BE CRUCIFIED.

Upon this Pilate sought to release him : but the Jews cried
out, saying, If thou release this man, thou art not Cæsar's
friend : every one that maketh himself a king speaketh
against Cæsar. When Pilate therefore heard these words,
he brought Jesus out, and sat down on the judgement-seat at
a place called The Pavement, but in Hebrew, Gabbatha.
Now it was the Preparation of the passover : it was about
the sixth hour. And he saith unto the Jews, Behold, your

---

1. John 19 : 6-11.

King! They therefore cried out, Away with *him*, away with *him*, crucify him.   Pilate saith unto them, Shall I crucify your King?   The chief priests answered, We have no king but Cæsar.¹   So when Pilate saw that he prevailed nothing, but rather that a tumult was arising, he took water, and washed his hands before the multitude, saying, I am innocent of the blood of this righteous man: see ye *to it.* And all the people answered and said, His blood *be* on us, and on our children.²   And Pilate, wishing to content the multitude [released unto them Barabbas]³, gave sentence that what they asked for should be done.   And he released him that for insurrection and murder had been cast into prison, whom they asked for; but Jesus he delivered up to their will,⁴ when he had scourged him, to be crucified.⁵

Then the soldiers of the governor took Jesus into the palace⁶ within the court which is called the Prætorium,⁷ and gathered unto him the whole band.   And they stripped him, and put on him a scarlet robe.   And they plaited a crown of thorns and put it upon his head, and a reed in his right hand; and they kneeled-down before him, and mocked him, saying, Hail, King of the Jews!   And they spat upon him, and took the reed and smote him on the head,⁸ and bowing their knees worshipped him.   And when they had mocked him, they took off from him the purple, and put on him his garments.   And they led him out to crucify him.⁹

·[He went out] bearing the cross for himself,¹⁰* and they led him away.¹¹   And as they came out, they found a man of Cyrene, Simon by name,¹² coming from the country, the father of Alexander and Rufus;¹³ him they compelled to go *with them*, that he might bear his cross.¹⁴

And there followed him a great multitude of the people, and of women who bewailed and lamented him.   But Jesus turning unto them said, Daughters of Jerusalem, weep not

---

1. John 19 : 12-15.
2. Matt. 27: 24, 25.
3. Mark 15 : 15.
4. Luke 23 : 24, 25.
5. Mark 15 : 15.
6. Matt. 27 : 27.
7. Mark 15 : 16.
8. Matt. 27 : 27-30.
9. Mark 15 : 19, 20.
10. John 19 : 17.
11. Luke 23 : 26.
12. Matt. 27 : 32.
13. Mark 15 : 21.
14. Matt. 27 : 32.

* " At first ; and when the weight was seen to be more than he could bear, Simon was compelled to bear it."—*Waddy.*

12

for me, but weep for yourselves, and for your chi'dren. For behold, the days are coming, in which they shall say, Blessed are the barren, and the wombs that never bare, and the breasts that never gave suck. Then shall they begin to say to the mountains, Fall on us; and to the hills, Cover us. For if they do these things in the green tree, what shall be done in the dry?[1]

And there were also two others, malefactors, led with him to be put to death.[2]

And when they were come unto a place,[3] which is called in Hebrew, Golgotha,[4] which is, being interpreted, The place of a skull,[5] they gave him wine to drink mingled with gall[6] [myrrh[7]]: and when he had tasted it he would not drink.[8]

§ 126—THE CRUCIFIXION.

And it was the third hour, and they crucified him. And with him they crucify two robbers, one on his right hand and one on his left,[9] and Jesus in the midst.[10] And Jesus said, Father, forgive them, for they know not what they do.[11]

The soldiers therefore, when they had crucified Jesus, took his garments, and made four parts, to every soldier a part; and also the coat: now the coat was without seam, woven from the top throughout. They said, therefore, one to another, Let us not rend it, but cast lots for it, whose it shall be: that the scripture might be fulfilled, which saith,

They parted my garments among them,
And upon my vesture did they cast lots.

These things therefore, the soldiers did.[12] And they sat and watched him there.[13]

And Pilate wrote a title also, •and put it on the cross. And there was written, JESUS OF NAZARETH, THE KING OF

---

1. Luke 23 : 27-31.	6. Matt. 27 : 34.	10. John 19 : 18.
2. Luke 23 : 32.	7. Mark 15 : 23.	11. Luke 23 : 34.
3. Matt. 27 : 33.	8. Matt. 27 : 34.	12. John 19 : 23, 24.
4. John 19 : 17,	9. Mark 15 : 25 and 27.	13. Matt. 27 : 36.
5. Mark 15 : 22.		

THE JEWS. This title therefore read many of the Jews : for the place where Jesus was crucified was nigh to the city : and it was written in Hebrew, *and* in Latin, *and* in Greek. The chief priests of the Jews therefore said to Pilate, Write not, The King of the Jews : but, that he said, I am King of the Jews. Pilate answered, What I have written I have written.[1]

But there were standing by the cross of Jesus his mother, and his mother's sister, Mary the *wife* of Clopas, and Mary Magdalene. When Jesus therefore saw his mother, and the disciple standing by, whom he loved, he saith unto his mother, Woman, behold, thy son ! Then saith he to the disciple, Behold, thy mother ! And from that hour the disciple took her unto his own *home.*[2]

And they that passed by railed on him, wagging their heads, and saying, Ha ! Thou that destroyest the temple, and buildest it in three days, save thyself[3] : if thou art the Son of God, come down from the cross. In like manner also the chief priests mocking *him,*[4] scoffed at him,[5] with the scribes and elders, said,[6] Let him save himself, if this is the Christ of God his chosen.[7] He saved others ; himself he cannot save. He is the King of Israel ; let him now come down from the cross, and we will believe on him. He trusteth on God ; let him deliver him now, if he desireth him : for he said, I am the Son of God.[8] And the soldiers also mocked him, coming to him, offering him vinegar, and saying, If thou art the King of the Jews, save thyself.[9] And the robbers also that were crucified with him cast upon him the same reproach.[10]

And one of the malefactors which were hanged railed on him, saying, Art not thou the Christ ? save thyself and us. But the other answered, and rebuking him said, Dost thou not even fear God, seeing thou art in the same condemnation ? And we indeed justly ; for we receive the due reward of our deeds : but this man hath done nothing amiss. And

---

1. John 19 : 19-22.
2. John 19 : 25-27.
3. Mark 15 : 29, 30.
4. Matt. 27 : 40, 41.
5. Luke 23 : 35.
6. Matt. 27 : 41.
7. Luke 23 : 35.
8. Matt. 27 : 42, 43.
9. Luke 23 : 36, 37.
10. Matt. 27 : 44.

he said, Jesus, remember me when thou comest in thy
kingdom.   And he said unto him, Verily I say unto thee,
To-day shalt thou be with me in Paradise.[1]

And when the sixth hour was come, there was darkness
over the whole land until the ninth hour,[2] the sun's light
failing.[3]   And at the ninth hour Jesus cried with a loud
voice, Eloi, Eloi, lama sabachthani? which is, being interpreted, My God, my God, why hast thou forsaken me?   And
some of them that stood by, when they heard it, said, Behold, he calleth Elijah.[4]

After this Jesus, knowing that all things are now finished,
that the scripture might be accomplished, saith, I thirst.
There was set there a vessel full of vinegar : so they put a
sponge full of the vinegar upon hyssop,[5] on a reed,[6] and
brought it to his mouth[7] and gave him to drink.   And the
rest said, Let be ; let us see whether Elijah cometh to save
him[8] [whether Elijah cometh to take him down[9]].   When
Jesus therefore had received the vinegar, he said, It is finished.[10]   And when Jesus had cried with a loud voice, he said,
Father, into thy hands I commend my spirit : and having
said this,[11] he bowed his head,[12] and yielded up his spirit[13]
[and gave up the ghost[14]].

And behold, the veil of the temple was rent in twain from
the top to the bottom ; and the earth did quake ; and the
rocks were rent; and the tombs were opened; and many
bodies of the saints that had fallen asleep were raised ; and
coming forth out of the tombs after his resurrection they
entered into the holy city and appeared unto many.   Now
the centurion, and they that were with him watching Jesus,
when they saw the earthquake, and the things that were
done, feared exceedingly, saying, Truly this was the Son of
God.[15]

[And when the centurion saw what was done, he glorified
God, saying, Certainly this was a righteous man.[16]]   And

1. Luke 23 : 39-43.   7. John 19 : 29.   12. John 19 : 30.
2. Mark 15 : 33.   8. Matt. 27 : 48, 49.   13. Matt. 27 : 50.
3. Luke 23 : 45.   9. Mark 15 : 36.   14. Mark 15 : 37.
4. Mark 15 : 34, 35.   10. John 19 : 30.   15. Matt. 27 : 51-54.
5. John 19 : 28, 29.   11. Luke 23 : 46.   16. Luke 23 : 47.
6. Matt. 27 : 48.

many women were there beholding from afar, which had followed Jesus from Galilee, ministering unto him :[1] [And all his acquaintance, and the women that followed with him from Galilee, stood afar off, seeing these things.] among whom *were* both Mary Magdalene, and Mary the mother of James the less and of Joses, and Salome ; who, when he was in Galilee, followed him, and ministered unto him : and many other women which came up with him unto Jerusalem.[3] And all the multitudes that came together to this sight, when they beheld the things that were done, returned smiting their breasts.[4]

The Jews therefore, because it was the Preparation, that the bodies should not remain on the cross upon the sabbath (for the day of that sabbath was a high *day*), asked of Pilate that their legs might be broken, and *that* they might be taken away. The soldiers therefore came, and brake the legs of the first, and of the other which was crucified with him : but when they came to Jesus, and saw that he was dead already, they brake not his legs : howbeit one of the soldiers with a spear pierced his side, and straightway there came out blood and water. And he that hath seen hath borne witness, and his witness is true : and he knoweth that he saith true, that ye also may believe. For these things came to pass, that the scripture might be fulfilled, A bone of him shall not be broken. And again another scripture saith, They shall look on him whom they pierced.[5]

§ 127—THE BURIAL OF JESUS.

And when even was now come, because it was the Preparation, that is, the day before the sabbath, there came Joseph [of Arimathæa,[6] a rich man[7]], a councillor of honourable estate,[8] a good man and a righteous (he had not consented to their counsel and deed), *a man* of Arimathæa, a city of the Jews,[9] who also himself was looking for the kingdom of God,[10]

---

1. Matt. 27 : 55.
2. Luke 23 : 49.
3. Mark 15 : 40, 41.
4. Luke 23 : 48.

5. John 19 : 31-37.
6. Mark 15 : 42, 43.
7. Matt. 27 : 57.

8. Mark 15 : 43.
9. Luke 23 : 50, 51.
10. Mark 15 : 43.

being a disciple of Jesus, but secretly for fear of the Jews,[1] and he boldly went in unto Pilate, and asked[2] that he might take away[3] the body of Jesus. And Pilate marvelled if he were already dead : and calling unto him the centurion, he asked him whether he had been any while dead. And when he learned it of the centurion, he granted the corpse to Joseph.[4] [Then Pilate commanded it to be given up.[5]] He came therefore, and took away his body. And there came also Nicodemus, he who at the first came to him by night, bringing a mixture of myrrh and aloes, about a hundred pound *weight*. So they took the body of Jesus, and bound it in linen cloths with the spices, as the custom of the Jews is to bury. Now in the place where he was crucified there was a garden ; and in the garden a new tomb wherein was never man yet laid.[6] And [Joseph] bought a linen cloth, and taking him down, wound him in the linen cloth, and laid him in[7] his own new tomb which he had hewn out of the rock, and he rolled a great stone to the door of the tomb and departed.[8]

[There then because of the Jews' Preparation (for the tomb was nigh at hand) they laid Jesus.[9]]

And it was the day of the Preparation, and the sabbath drew on. And the women, which had come with him out of Galilee, followed after, and beheld the tomb, and how his body was laid.[10] [And Mary Magdalene was there, and the other Mary. sitting over against the sepulchre.[11]] And they returned, and prepared spices and ointments. And on the sabbath they rested according to the commandment.[12]

Now on the morrow, which is *the day* after the Preparation, the chief priests and the Pharisees were gathered together unto Pilate, saying, Sir, we remember that that deceiver said, while he was yet alive, After three days I rise again. Command therefore that the sepulchre be made sure until the third day, lest haply his disciples come and steal him away, and say unto the people, He is risen from

---

1. John 19 : 38.	5. Matt. 27 : 58.	9. John 19 : 42.
2. Mark 15 : 43.	6. John 19 : 38-41.	10. Luke 23 : 54, 55.
3. John 19 : 38.	7. Mark 15 : 46.	11. Matt. 27 : 61.
4. Mark 15 : 43-45.	8. Matt. 27 : 60.	12. Luke 23 : 56.

the dead : and the last error will be worse than the first. Pilate said unto them, Ye have a guard : go your way, make it *as* sure as ye can. So they went, and made the sepulchre sure, sealing the stone, the guard being with them.[1]

§ 128 —THE RESURRECTION OF JESUS.

Matt. 28 : 1-8.	Mark 16 : 1-8.
Now late on the sabbath day, as it began to dawn toward the first *day* of the week, came Mary Magdalene and the other ·Mary to see the sepulchre. And behold, there was a great earthquake; for an angel of the Lord descended from heaven, and came and rolled away the stone, and sat upon it. His appearance was as lightning, and his raiment white ·as snow: and for fear of him the watchers did quake, and became as dead men. And the angel answered and said unto the women, Fear not ye : for I know that ye seek Jesus, which hath been crucified. He is not here ; for he is risen, even as he said. Come, see the place where the Lord lay. And go quickly, and tell his disciples, He is risen from the dead; and lo, he goeth before you into Galilee; there shall ye see him : lo, I have told you. And they departed	And when the sabbath was past, Mary Magdalene, and Mary the *mother* of James, and Salome, bought spices, that they might come and anoint him. And very early on the first day of the week, they come to the tomb when the sun was risen. And they were saying among themselves, Who shall roll us away the stone from the door of the tomb ? and looking up, they see that the stone is rolled back : for it was exceeding great. And entering into the tomb, they saw a young man sitting on the right side, arrayed in a white robe; and they were amazed. And he saith unto them, Be not a-mazed : ye seek Jesus, the Nazarene, which hath been crucified : he is risen; he is not here : behold, the place where they laid him ! But go, tell his disciples and Peter, He goeth before you into

---

1 Matt. 27 : 62-66.

quickly from the tomb with fear and great joy, and ran to bring his disciples word.

Galilee: there shall ye see him, as he said unto you. And they went out, and fled from the tomb; for trembling and astonishment had come upon them: and they said nothing to any one; for they were afraid.

Luke 23 : 56 ; 24 : 1-12.

And on the sabbath they rested according to the commandment. But on the first day of the week, at early dawn, they came unto the tomb, bringing the spices which they had prepared. And they found the stone rolled away from the tomb. And they entered in, and found not the body of the Lord Jesus. And it came to pass, while they were perplexed thereabout, behold, two men stood by them in dazzling apparel: and as they were affrighted, and bowed down their faces to the earth, they said unto them, Why seek ye the living among the dead ? He is not here, but is risen: remember how he spake unto you when he was yet in Galilee, saying that the Son of man must be delivered up into the hands of sinful men, and be crucified, and the third day rise again. And they remembered his words,

John 20 : 1-10.

Now on the first *day* of the week cometh Mary Magdalene early, while it was yet dark, unto the tomb, and seeth the stone taken away from the tomb. She runneth therefore, and cometh to Simon Peter, and to the other disciple, whom Jesus loved, and saith unto them, They have taken away the Lord out of the tomb, and we know not where they have laid him. Peter therefore went forth, and the other disciple, and they went toward the tomb. And they ran both together: and the other disciple outran Peter, and came first to the tomb; and stooping and looking in, he seeth the linen clohts lying; yet entered he not in. Simon Peter therefore also cometh, following him, and entered into the tomb; and he beholdeth the linen cloths lying, and the napkin, that was upon his head, not lying with the linen cloths, but

and returned from the tomb, and told all these things to the eleven, and to all the rest. Now they were Mary Magdalene, and Joanna, and Mary the *mother* of James: and the other women with them told these things unto the apostles. And these words appeared in their sight as idle talk; and they disbelieved them. But Peter arose, and ran unto the tomb; and stooping and looking in, he seeth the linen cloths by themselves; and he departed to his home, wondering at that which was come to pass.

rolled up in a place by itself. Then entered in therefore the other disciple also, which came first to the tomb, and he saw, and believed. For as yet they knew not the scripture, that he must rise again from the dead. So the disciples went away again unto their own home.

§ 129—JESUS APPEARS (1) TO MARY MAGDALENE, (2) TO MARY MAGDALENE AND THE "OTHER MARY."

But Mary was standing without at the tomb weeping: so, as she wept, she stooped and looked into the tomb; and she beholdeth two angels in white sitting, one at the head, and one at the feet, where the body of Jesus had lain. And they say unto her, Woman, why weepest thou? She saith unto them, Because they have taken away my Lord, and I know not where they have laid him. When she had thus said, she turned herself back, and beholdeth Jesus standing, and knew not that it was Jesus. Jesus saith unto her, Woman, why weepest thou? whom seekest thou? She, supposing him to be the gardener, saith unto him, Sir, if thou hast borne him hence, tell me where thou hast laid him, and I[1]

---

1. John 20 : 11-15.

will take him away. Jesus saith unto her, Mary. She turn-
eth herself, and saith unto him in Hebrew, Rabboni; which
is to say, Master. Jesus saith to her, Touch me not; for
I am not yet ascended unto the Father: but go unto my
brethren, and say to them, I ascend unto my Father and
your Father, and my God and your God. Mary Magdalene
cometh and telleth the disciples, I have seen the Lord; and
how that he had said these things unto her.[1]

[Now when he was risen early on the first day of the
week, he appeared first to Mary Magdalene, from whom he
had cast out seven devils. She went and told them that had
been with him, as they mourned and wept. And they,
when they heard that he was alive, and had been seen of
her, disbelieved.[2]]

And behold, Jesus met them,* saying, All hail. And
they came and took hold of his feet, and worshipped him.
Then saith Jesus unto them, Fear not: go tell my brethren
that they depart into Galilee, and there shall they see me.[3]

§ 130—THE GUARDS GIVE A FALSE ACCOUNT OF THE DISAPPEARANCE OF THE BODY OF JESUS.

Now while they were going, behold, some of the guard
came into the city, and told unto the chief priests all the
things that were come to pass. And when they were assembled with the elders, and had taken counsel, they gave large
money unto the soldiers, saying, Say ye, His disciples came
by night, and stole him away while we slept. And if this
come to the governor's ears, we will persuade him, and rid
you of care. So they took the money, and did as they were
taught: and this saying was spread abroad among the Jews,
and continueth until this day.[4]

---

1. John 20: 15-18.   3. Matt. 28 : 9, 10.   4. Matt. 28 : 11-15.
2. Mark 16: 9-11.

* That is, "Mary Magdalene and the other Mary." See Matt. 28: 1-8.—
Waddy.

§ 131—JESUS APPEARS (3) TO THE DISCIPLES ON THE WAY TO EMMAUS.

And after these things he was manifested in another form unto two of them, as they walked on their way into the country.[1]

And behold, two of them were going that very day to a village named Emmaus, which was threescore furlongs from Jerusalem. And they communed with each other of all these things which had happened. And it came to pass, while they communed and questioned together, that Jesus himself drew near, and went with them. But their eyes were holden that they should not know him. And he said unto them, What communications are these that ye have one with another, as ye walk? And they stood still, looking sad. And one of them, named Cleopas, answering said unto him, Dost thou alone sojourn in Jerusalem and not know the things which are come to pass there in these days? And he said unto them, What things? And they said unto him, The things concerning Jesus of Nazareth, which was a prophet mighty in deed and word before God and all the people: and how the chief priests and our rulers delivered him up to be condemned to death, and crucified him. But we hoped that it was he which should redeem Israel. Yea and beside all this, it is now the third day since these things came to pass. Moreover certain women of our company amazed us, having been early at the tomb; and when they found not his body, they came, saying, that they had also seen a vision of angels, which said that he was alive. And certain of them that were with us went to the tomb, and found it even so as the women had said: but him they saw not. And he said unto them, O foolish men, and slow of heart to believe in all that the prophets have spoken! Behoved it not the Christ to suffer these things, and to enter into his glory? And beginning from Moses and from all the prophets, he interpreted to them in all the scriptures the[2]

---

1. Mark 16 : 12.   2. Luke 24 : 13-27.

things concerning himself. And they drew nigh unto the
village, whither they were going: and he made as though he
would go further. And they constrained him, saying, Abide
with us: for it is toward evening, and the day is now far
spent. And he went in to abide with them.

And it came to pass, when he had sat down with them to
meat, he took the bread, and blessed it, and brake, and
gave to them. And their eyes were opened, and they knew
him; and he vanished out of their sight. And they said
one to another, Was not our heart burning within us, while
he spake to us in the way, while he opened to us the
scriptures?[1]

§ 132—JESUS APPEARS (4) TO PETER.

And they went away and told it unto the rest: neither
believed they them.[2]

And they rose up that very hour, and returned to Jerusalem, and found the eleven gathered together, and them
that were with them, saying, The Lord is risen indeed, and
hath appeared to Simon. And they rehearsed the things
that happened in the way, and how he was known of them
in the breaking of the bread.[3]

§ 133—JESUS APPEARS (5) TO THE DISCIPLES IN
THE ABSENCE OF THOMAS.

[I delivered unto you first of all that which also I received,
how that Christ died for our sins according to the scriptures;
and that he was buried; and that he hath been raised on
the third day according to the scriptures; and that he
appeared to Cephas; then to the twelve;[4] then to all the
apostles.[5]]

And afterward he was manifested unto the eleven themselves as they sat at meat.[6]

---

1. Luke 24: 27-32.   3. Luke 24: 33-35.   5. 1 Cor. 15: 7.
2. Mark 16: 13.   4. 1 Cor. 15: 3-5.   6. Mark 16: 14.

When therefore it was evening, on that day, the first *day* of the week, and when the doors were shut where the disciples were, for fear of the Jews, Jesus came and stood in the midst, and saith unto them, Peace *be* unto you.[1] But they were terrified and affrighted, and supposed that they beheld a spirit.[2] And he upbraided them with their unbelief and hardness of heart, because they believed not them which had seen him after he was risen.[3]

And he said unto them, Why are ye troubled? and wherefore do reasonings arise in your heart? See my hands and my feet, that it is I myself: handle me, and see; for a spirit hath not flesh and bones, as ye behold me having. And when he had said this, he shewed them his hands and his feet. And while they still disbelieved for joy, and wondered, he said unto them, Have ye here anything to eat? And they gave him a piece of a broiled fish. And he took it, and did eat before them.[4] The disciples therefore were glad, when they saw the Lord. Jesus therefore said to them again, Peace *be* unto you: as the Father hath sent me, even so send I you. And when he had said this, he breathed on them, and saith unto them, Receive ye the Holy Ghost: whose soever sins ye forgive, they are forgiven unto them; whose soever *sins* ye retain, they are retained.[5]

And he said unto them, These are my words which I spake unto you, while I was yet with you, how that all things must needs be fulfilled, which are written in the law of Moses, and the prophets, and the psalms, concerning me. Then opened he their mind, that they might understand the scriptures; and he said unto them, Thus it is written, that the Christ should suffer, and rise again from the dead the third day; and that repentance and remission of sins should be preached in his name unto all the nations, beginning from Jerusalem. Ye are witnesses of these things. And behold, I send forth the promise of my Father upon you: but tarry ye in the city, until ye be clothed with power from on high.[6]

---

1. John 20 : 19.   3. Mark 16 : 14.   5. John 20 : 20-23.
2. Luke 24 : 37.   4. Luke 24 : 38-43.   6. Luke 24 : 44-49.

And, being assembled together with them, he charged them not to depart from Jerusalem, but to wait for the promise of the Father, which, *said he*, ye heard from me: for John indeed baptized with water; but ye shall be baptized with the Holy Ghost not many days hence.[1]

§ 134—JESUS APPEARS (6) TO THE DISCIPLES
WHEN THOMAS IS PRESENT.

But Thomas, one of the twelve, called Didymus, was not with them when Jesus came. The other disciples therefore said unto him, We have seen the Lord. But he said unto them, Except I shall see in his hands the print of the nails, and put my finger into the print of the nails, and put my hand into his side, I will not believe.

And after eight days' again his disciples were within, and Thomas with them. Jesus cometh, the doors being shut, and stood in the midst, and said, Peace *be* unto you. Then saith he to Thomas, Reach hither thy finger, and see my hands; and reach *hither* thy hand, and put it into my side: and be not faithless, but believing. Thomas answered and said unto him, My Lord and my God. Jesus saith unto him, Because thou hast seen me, thou hast believed: blessed *are* they that have not seen, and *yet* have believed.[2]

§ 135—JESUS APPEARS (7) TO THE DISCIPLES AT THE
SEA OF GALILEE.

After these things Jesus manifested himself again to the disciples at the sea of Tiberias ; and he manifested *himself* on this wise. There were together Simon Peter, Thomas called Didymus, and Nathanael of Cana in Galilee, and the *sons* of Zebedee, and two other of his disciples. Simon Peter saith unto them, I go a fishing. They say unto him, We also come with thee. They went forth, and entered into the boat ; and that night they took nothing.[3] But when day

---

1. Acts 1 : 4, 5.　　2. John 20 : 24-29.　　3. John 21: 1-3.

was now breaking, Jesus stood on the beach : howbeit the disciples knew not that it was Jesus. Jesus therefore saith unto them, Children, have ye aught to eat? They answered him, No. And he said unto them, Cast the net on the right side of the boat, and ye shall find. They cast therefore, and now they were not able to draw it for the multitude of fishes. That disciple therefore whom Jesus loved saith unto Peter, It is the Lord. So when Simon Peter heard that it was the Lord, he girt his coat about him (for he was naked), and cast himself into the sea. But the other disciples came in the little boat (for they were not far from the land, but about two hundred cubits off), dragging the net *full* of fishes. So when they got out upon the land, they see a fire of coals there, and fish laid thereon, and bread. Jesus saith unto them, Bring of the fish which ye have now taken. Simon Peter therefore went up, and drew the net to land, full of great fishes, a hundred and fifty and three : and for all there was so many, the net was not rent. Jesus saith unto them, Come *and* break your fast. And none of the disciples durst inquire of him, Who art thou? knowing that it was the Lord. Jesus cometh, and taketh the bread, and giveth them, and the fish likewise. This is now the third time that Jesus was manifested to the disciples, after that he was risen from the dead.

So when they had broken their fast, Jesus saith to Simon Peter, Simon, *son* of John, lovest thou me more than these? He saith unto him, Yea, Lord ; thou knowest that I love thee. He saith unto him, Feed my lambs. He saith to him again a second time, Simon, *son* of John, lovest thou me? He saith unto him, Yea, Lord ; thou knowest that I love thee. He saith unto him, Tend my sheep. He saith unto him the third time, Simon, *son* of John, lovest thou me? Peter was grieved because he said unto him the third time, Lovest thou me? And he said unto him, Lord, thou knowest all things ; thou knowest that I love thee. Jesus saith unto him, Feed my sheep. Verily, verily, I say unto thee, When thou wast young, thou girdedst thyself,[1] and

1. John 21 : 4-18.

walkedst whither thou wouldest: but when thou shalt be old,
thou shalt stretch forth thy hands, and another shall gird
thee, and carry thee whither thou wouldest not.   Now this
he spake, signifying by what manner of death he should
glorify God.   And when he had spoken this, he saith unto
them, Follow me.   Pet r, turning about, seeth the disciple
whom Jesus loved following ; which also leaned back on his
breast at the supper, and said, Lord, who is he that betrayeth thee ?   Peter therefore seeing him saith to Jesus, Lord,
and what shall this man do ?   Jesus saith unto him, If I will
that he tarry till I come, what *is that* to thee ? follow thou
me.   This saying therefore went forth among the brethren,
that that disciple should not die : yet Jesus said not unto
him, that he should not die ; but, If I will that he tarry till
I come, what *is that* to thee ?

  This is the disciple which beareth witness of these things,
and wrote these things, and we know that his witness is
true.[1]

§ 136—JESUS APPEARS (8) AGAIN TO THE DISCIPLES,
(9) TO THE FIVE HUNDRED, (10) TO JAMES,
THE LORD'S BROTHER.

But the eleven disciples went into Galilee, unto the mountain where Jesus had appointed them.   And when they saw
him, they worshipped *him* : but some doubted.   And Jesus
came to them and spake unto them, saying, All authority
hath been given unto me in heaven and on earth.[2]   And he
said unto them, Go ye into all the world, and preach the
gospel to the whole creation,[3] and make disciples of all the
nations, baptizing them in the name of the Father and of the
Son and of the Holy Ghost : teaching them to observe all
things whatsoever I commanded you.[4]

He that believeth and is baptized shall be saved ; but he
that disbelieveth shall be condemned.   And these signs shall

---

1. John 21 : 18-24.   3. Mark 16 : 15.   4. Matt. 28 : 19, 20.
2. Matt. 28 : 16-18.

follow them that believe : in my name shall they cast out
devils ; they shall speak with new tongues ; they shall take
up serpents, and if they drink any deadly thing, it shall in
no wise hurt them ; they shall lay hands on the sick, and
they shall recover.[1]

And lo, I am with you alway, even unto the end of the
world.[2]

Then he appeared to above five hundred brethren at once,
of whom the greater part remain until now, but some are
fallen asleep ; then he appeared to James ; then to all the
apostles,[3] to whom he also shewed himself alive after his
passion by many proofs, appearing unto them by the space
of forty days, and speaking the things concerning the
kingdom of God.[4] And last of all, as unto one born out of
due time, he appeared to me also.[5]

§ 137—THE ASCENSION OF JESUS.

And he led them out until they were over against
Bethany,[6] [at] the mount called Olivet, which is nigh unto
Jerusalem.

They therefore, when they were come together, asked
him, saying, Lord, dost thou at this time restore the kingdom to Israel ? And he said unto them, It is not for you to
know times or seasons, which the Father hath set within
his own authority. But ye shall receive power, when the
Holy Ghost is come upon you : and ye shall be my witnesses
both in Jerusalem, and in all Judæa and Samaria, and unto
the uttermost part of the earth. And when he had said
these things,[8] he lifted up his hands, and blessed them.
And it came to pass, while he blessed them,[9] as they were
looking,[10] he parted from them and was carried up into
heaven,[11] and a cloud received him out of their sight,[12] and
[he] sat down at the right hand of God.[13]

---

1. Mark 16 : 16-18.
2. Matt. 28 : 20.
3. 1 Cor. 15 : 6, 7.
4. Acts 1 : 3.
5. 1 Cor. 15 : 8.
6. Luke 24 : 50.
7. Acts 1 : 12.
8. Acts 1 : 6-9.
9. Luke 24 : 50, 51.
10. Acts 1 : 9.
11. Luke 24 : 51.
12. Acts 1 : 9.
13. Mark 16 : 19.

13

And while they were looking stedfastly into heaven as he went, behold, two men stood by them in white apparel; which also said, Ye men of Galilee, why stand ye looking into heaven? this Jesus, which was received up from you into heaven, shall so come in like manner as ye beheld him going into heaven.[1] And they worshipped him, and returned to Jerusalem with great joy: and were continually in the temple, blessing God.[2] And they went forth, and preached everywhere, the Lord working with them, and confirming the word by the signs that followed. Amen.[3]

Many other signs therefore did Jesus in the presence of the disciples, which are not written in this book: but these are written, that ye may believe that Jesus is the Christ, the Son of God; and that believing ye may have life in his name.[4]

And there are also many other things which Jesus did, the which if they should be written every one, I suppose that even the world itself would not contain the books that should be written.

---

1. Acts 1 : 10, 11.   3. Mark 16 : 20.   5. John 21 : 25.
2. Luke 24 : 52, 53.   4. John 20 : 30, 31.